In memory of Kathleen...

Edited by Sacha Llewellyn, Paul Liss and George Richards

British Drawings
1890 - 1990

Exhibition to be held at:
SOTHERAN'S
2 Sackville Street
London W1S 3DP
7- 28 OCTOBER 2022

For all enquiries
please contact
George Richards:
george@lissllewellyn.com
+44 (0)7497 492756

LISS LLEWELLYN

Sotheran's
EST. LONDON 1761

Purdy | Hicks

Introduction

"I prefer drawing to talking. Drawing is faster, and leaves less room for lies." – Le Corbusier

'Drawings' is a collaborative venture combining two exhibitions that have been timed to coincide: ***British Drawings: 1890-1990*** at Sotheran's, and ***Drawings 1990-2022*** at Purdy Hicks Gallery. Both shows emphasise the importance of drawing to artists of the last 120 years: though many of the artists have used myriad other art forms, they have invariably returned to the honesty of drawing, time and time again.

The artists reflect their times. The artists from 1890-1980 are very much associated with strong schools of thought. One school in particular, the Slade School of Fine Art, dominates. Its rigorous process of drawing underpins much that we see, but is of course interpreted differently artist by artist. There was most definitely a British School, and in terms of drawing its greatest, though largely unacknowledged, triumph can be found in the remarkable works produced by the artists of the British School at Rome with their use of drawing techniques dating back to the Renaissance. This catalogue contains outstanding examples by Winifred Knights, Evelyn Gibbs, Anne Newland, Thomas Monnington, Robert Austin, Alan Sorrell and Reginald Brill. Slade student Winifred Knights exemplified the teachings of Henry Tonks, (Professor of Fine Art at the Slade from 1918 to 1930), with her observation of nature and meticulous methodology, working through endless studies, which were in turn painstakingly transferred to create finished works. Gilbert Spencer, another of the Professor's students, recalled how Tonks «talked of dedication, the privilege of being an artist, that to do a bad drawing was like living with a lie, and he proceeded to implant these ideals by ruthless and withering criticism. I remember once coming home and feeling like flinging myself under a train, and Stan telling me not to mind as he did it to everyone.»

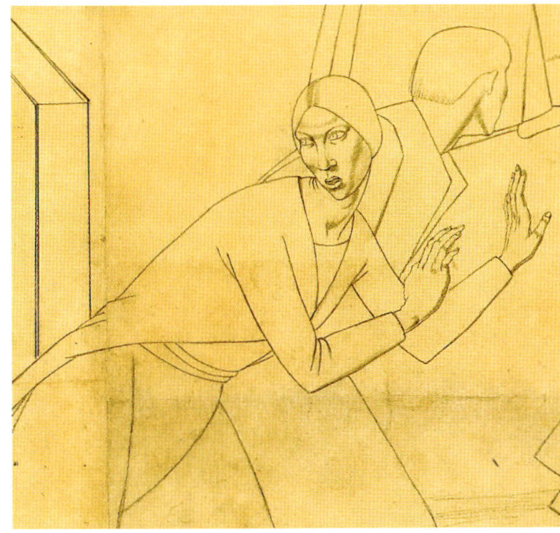

Methodology aside, many of the artists in this catalogue share common traits – an obsession with the minutiae of nature, an unbreakable attachment to landscape, an immersion in the narrative tradition, and an inability to resist humour and affection for the quirky and mundane.

The exhibition at Purdy Hicks, part two of this collaboration, shows that through the success of the School of London and the Young British Artists (YBA), who blossomed in the 80s and 90s, ideas of Britishness as a defining quality were soon discarded. London had become primarily an international centre, not a British one.

Drawing, unlike painting, somehow managed not to be dragged into the main ideological divide of the last century between Communism and Capitalism. The 'free West' fled into abstraction, and the Soviet Union countered with Soviet Realism. Here we have figurative works by Thomas Monnington, including a portrait of his now more famous wife, Winifred Knights, but he was also the first President of the Royal Academy to embrace abstraction. The drawings here of John Tunnard and Cecil Stephenson explore abstraction - but sneak under the radar. By the time we get to Gillian Ayres her works on paper are unequivocally abstract, with even the division between painting and drawing are blurring.

Not surprisingly two of the younger artists in the collaborative show at Purdy Hicks Post-80s show give the most contemporary take on Corbusier's boast for drawing. Olga Chernysheva and Waqas Khan have found very different ways to help heal the wounds of the abstract/figurative cold war.

The definition of drawing was definitely much tighter 120 years ago. There is a tendency among many contemporary artists and curators not to use the term, but rather categorise these works under the broad cover-all of works on paper. The fluidity in the terminology was different for the 19th and much of the 20th century. Here concepts about the line are of primary concern, but this allows 'drawing' to be seen in a wide range of media including etching and sketches in oil and tempera. All of the works in these two exhibitions however bear witness to the art of drawing and the challenge of the life-long journey that learning its art involves. As Ingres asserted, and not entirely in jest: 'It takes twenty-five years to learn to draw, one hour to learn to paint.'

Alistair Hicks

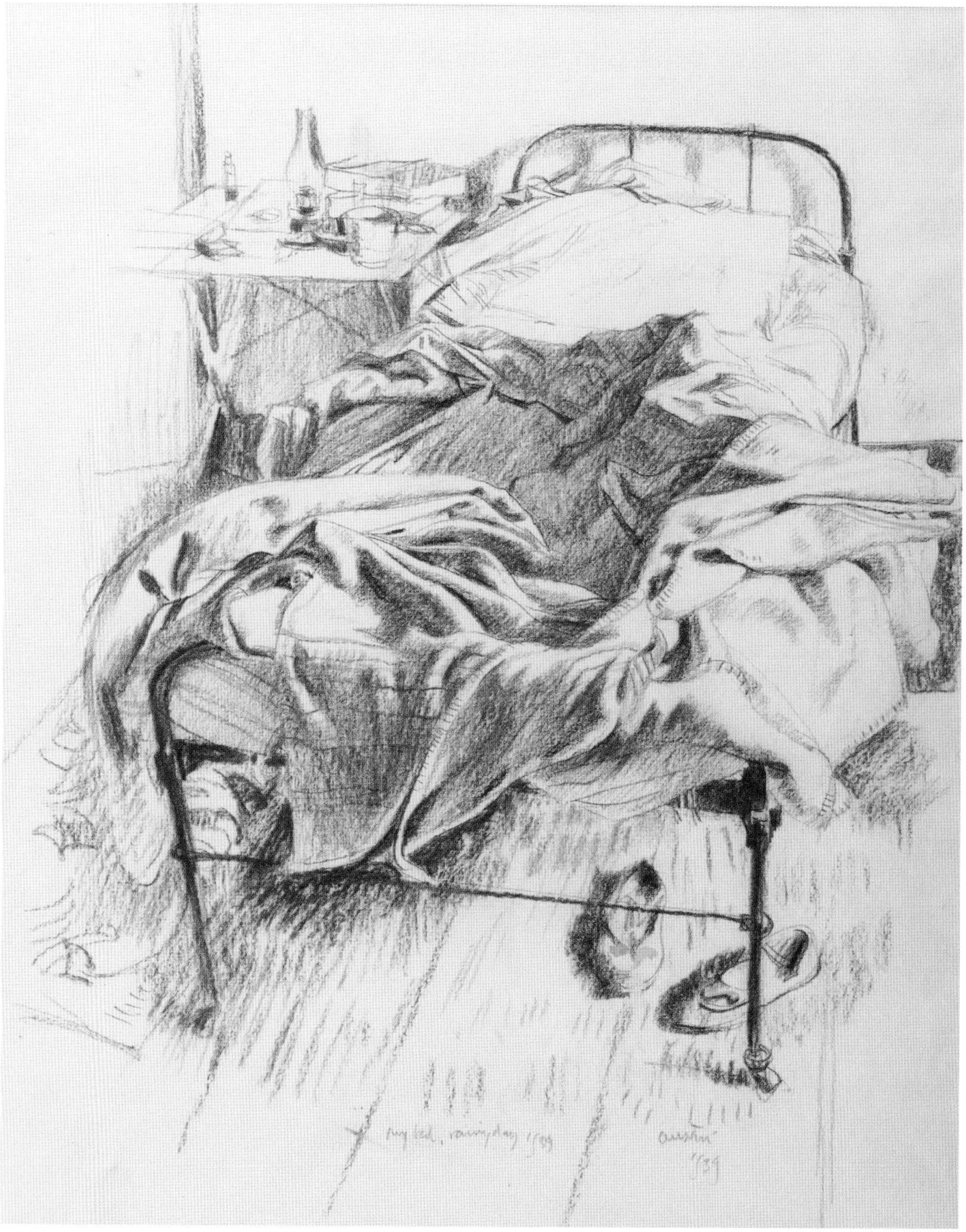
my bed, rainy day 1/39

Robert Austin (1895-1973)

My bed, rainy day, 1939

Signed and inscribed with title, dated twice, pencil, crayon, highlights in pink and green watercolour - 46.5 x 31 cm.

This evocative composition dates to the opening months of WW2 – a period during which Austin worked as an Official War Artist whilst also teaching at the (evacuated) Royal College of Art in Ambleside. In spite of requisitioning two hotels, conditions for the Royal College of Art students and staff were cramped. The majority of space was given over to accommodation leaving precious little room for artist's studios, which were mostly set up in lower rooms and suffered from lack of light. In the domestic routine, however, which formed the backdrop to his work, Austin found an endless source of inspiration. Drapery was a subject that he was particularly drawn to.

The majority of Austin's war work is in the Imperial War Museum.

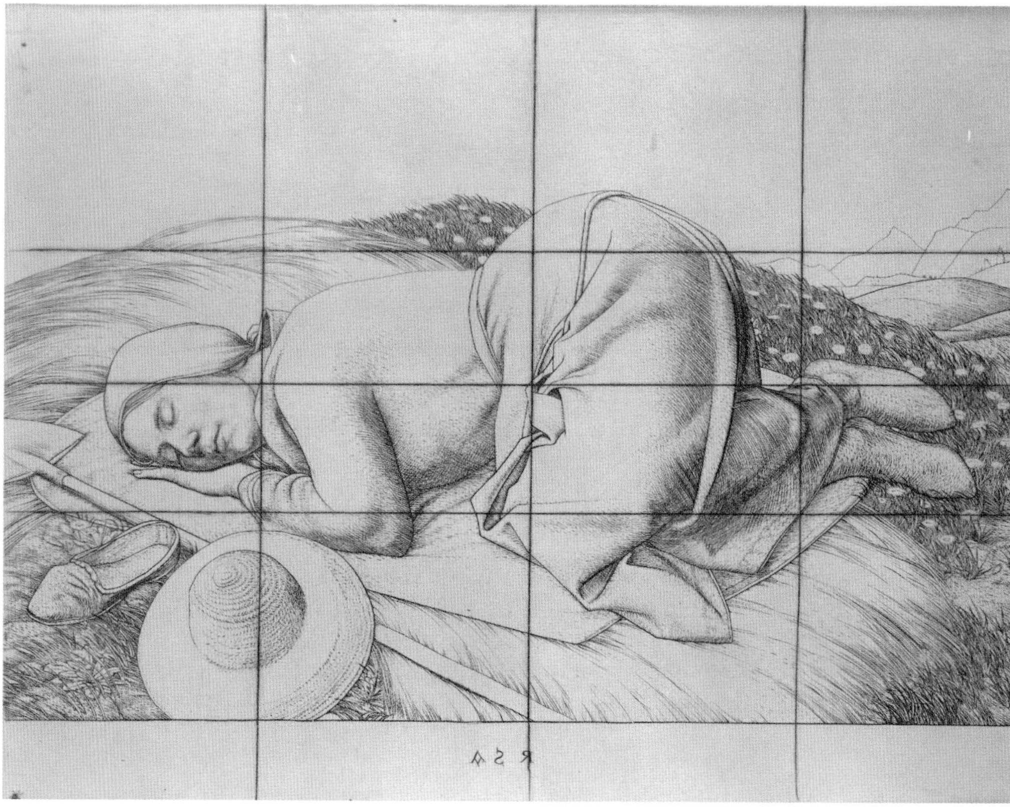

Robert Austin (1895-1973)

Midday rest, 1932

Signed with initials, the original steel-faced copper etching plate,with cancellation lines - 15 x 19.5 cm.

This original plate for one of Austin's most evocative etchings, *Midday*, encapsulates a memory typical of the type that left its mark on Austin during his three-year tenure at the British School at Rome, as Rome Scholar in Engraving from 1923-1926. During the summer months Italian peasants frequently took their siestas, or passed entire nights, sleeping in the open fields.

In *The English Print* (Adam and Charles Black 1937), Basil Gray enthused about Austin's 'sweetness of line' and ability to produce a 'unified composition', concluding that he was '*master not only of his technique, in which no English engraver has surpassed him, but also in using his medium in a native, personal way*'. It is generally acknowledged that Austin was one of the greatest exponents of line engraving of the 20th century. Campbell Dodgson, Keeper of Prints and Drawings at the British Museum, who compiled the standard reference work on Austin, compared his work to that of Durer, noting that *Austin had more than a touch of that master in him.*

(A Catalogue of Etchings and Engravings by Robert Austin, Twenty-One Gallery, London, 1930).

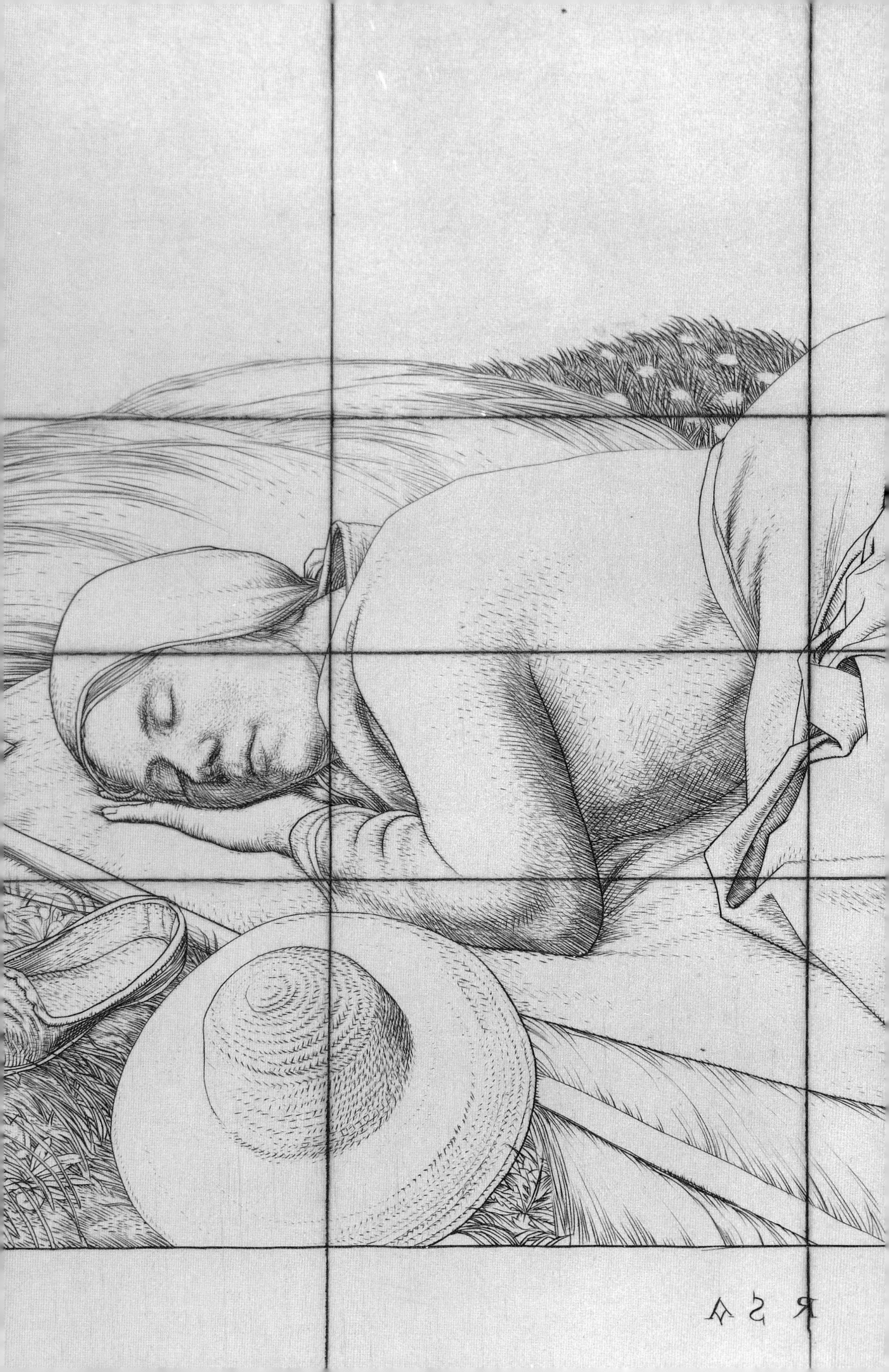

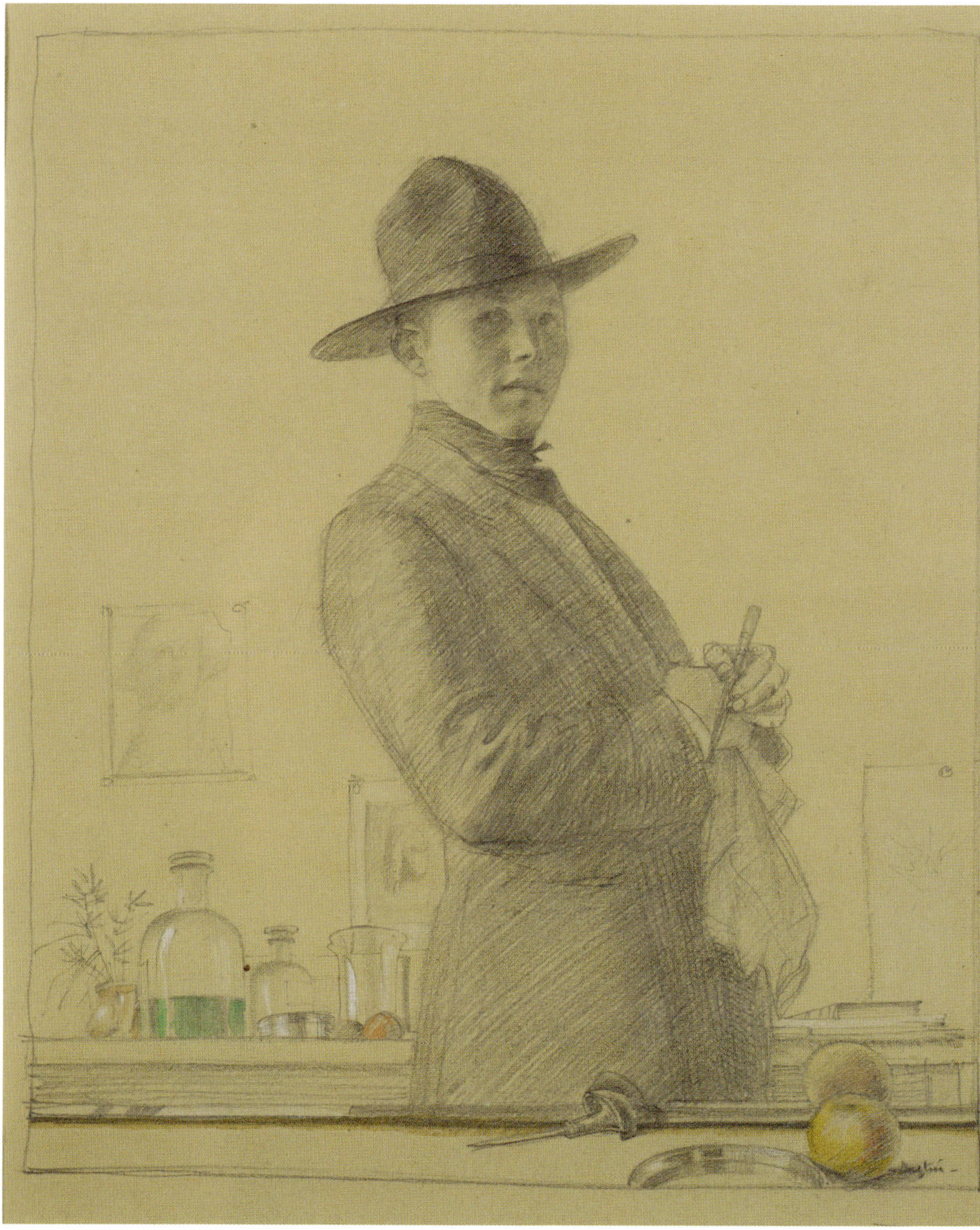

Robert Austin (1895-1973)

Self Portrait in Roman Hat, circa 1925

Signed, pencil and watercolour - 25.4 x 20.3 cm.

Proud of his status as winner of The Scholarship in Engraving at the British School at Rome for 1922, in this self-portrait Robert Austin portrays himself striking a 'swagger' pose and wearing a recently purchased Roman Hat. Holding an etching needle, a jar of green hydrochloric acid, used in the printing process, can be seen in the background, along with a burin, (used by engravers used to cut into an etching plate), which balances on the mantelpiece of the fire surround. The artist is surrounded by the tools of his trade.

This drawing was gifted by Austin to Eleanor Hudson, (Austin's student and mistress) a watercolourist, etcher and designer best known for her depictions of women at work during WW2.

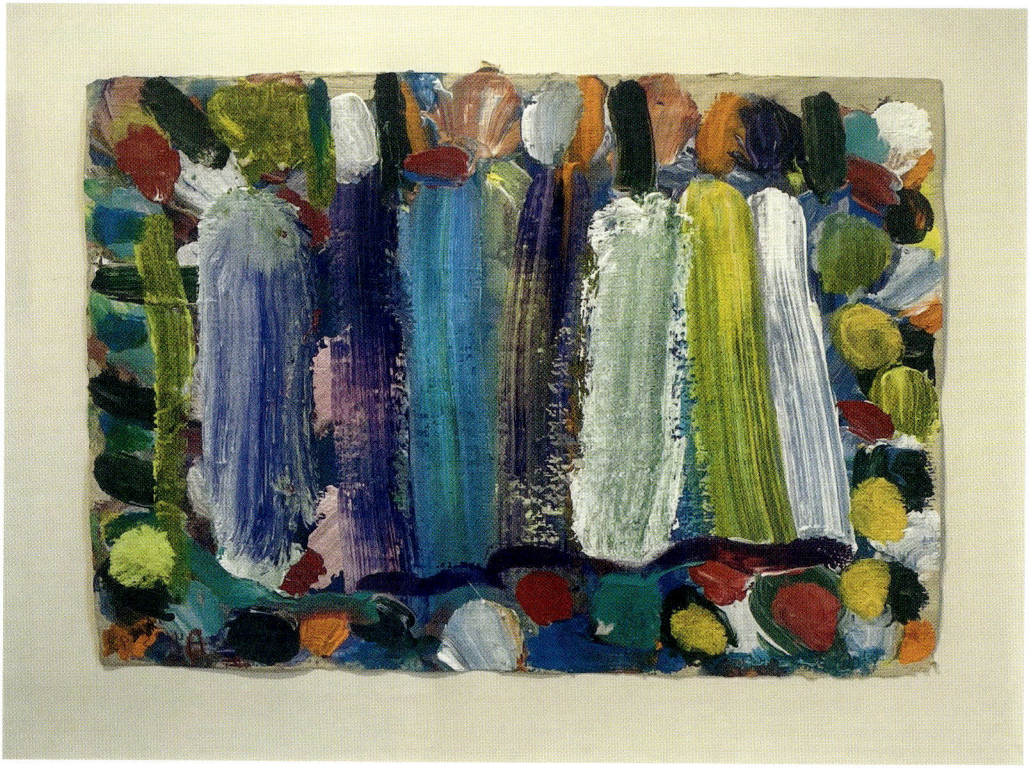

Gillian Ayres (1930-2018)

Untitled, 1993

Signed and dated, acrylic on paper - 40 x 57 cm.

This work is from a series inspired by a visit to Provence when the artist stayed with Frederick Gore.

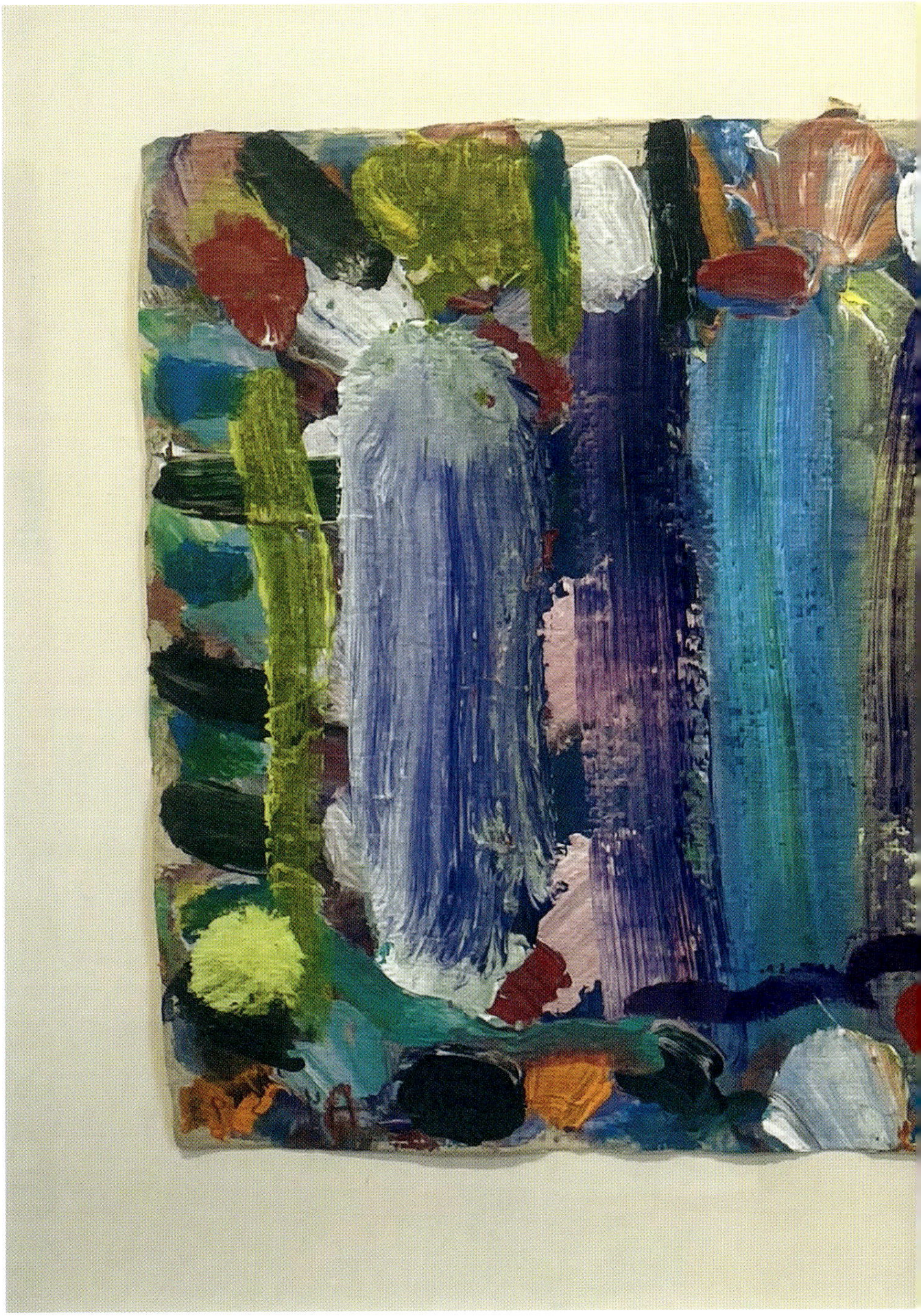

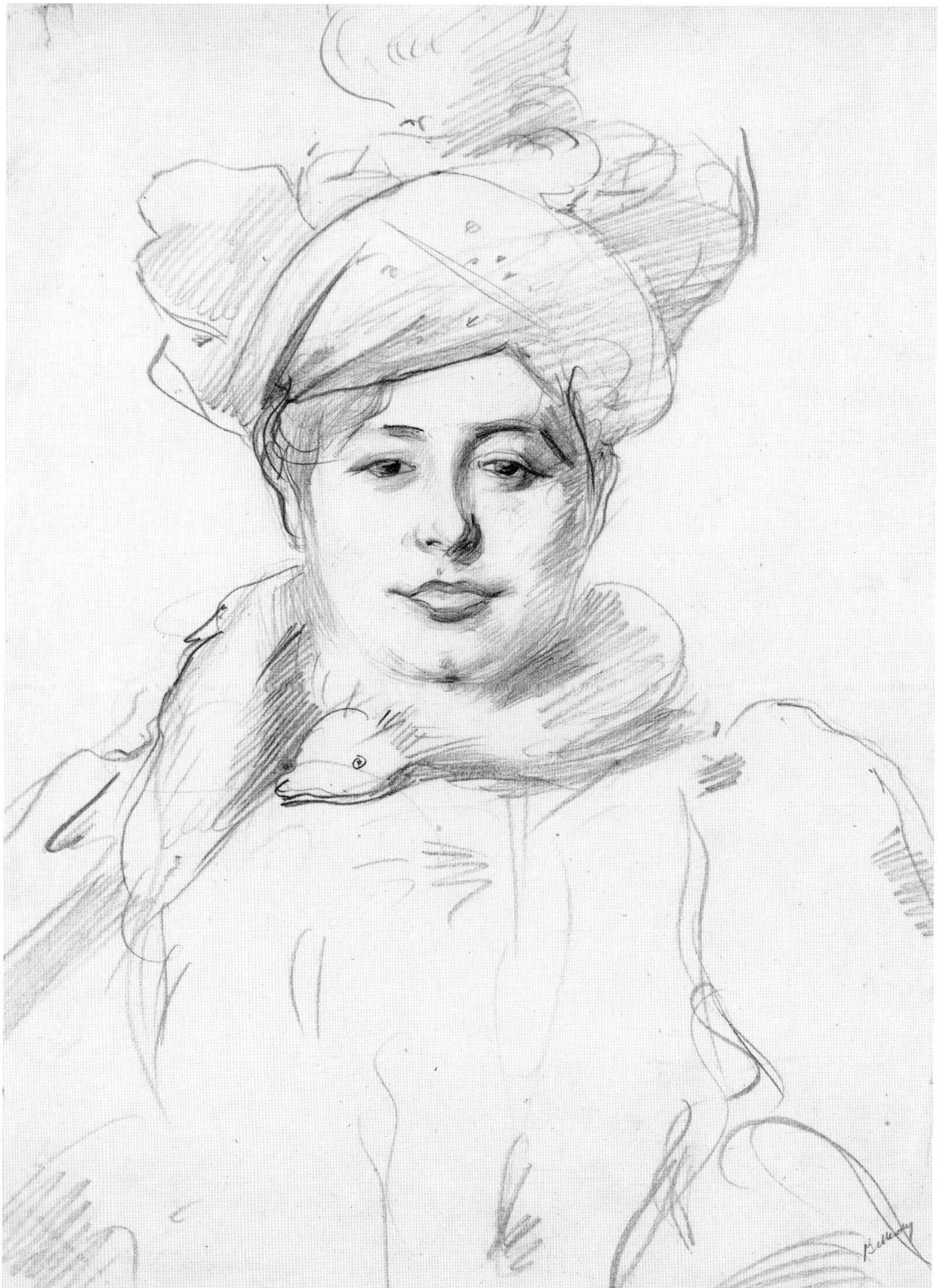

Albert de Belleroche (1864-1944)

Mata Hari, circa 1905

Pencil - 36.7 x 26 cm.

Mata Hari, a celebrated Dutch dancer, was part of the demi-monde frequented by Albert de Belleroche in Belle Epoque Paris during the decades leading up to and following the turn of the 20th century. She modelled several times for Belleroche and was the subject of several lithographs. Notoriously she was convicted of spying for the Germans during WW1 and executed by firing squad in France, in 1917.

Writing about Belleroche's prodigious talent for draughtsmanship, (in '*Peintres-lithographes Contemporains*', 1908), the influential critic Roger Marx observed: '*These are thoroughly modern works which capture brief, reverent moments of joy, tenderness and wonder, much like the works of Sargent, Helleu or Besnard. Belleroche's portraits of women are iconographic*'.

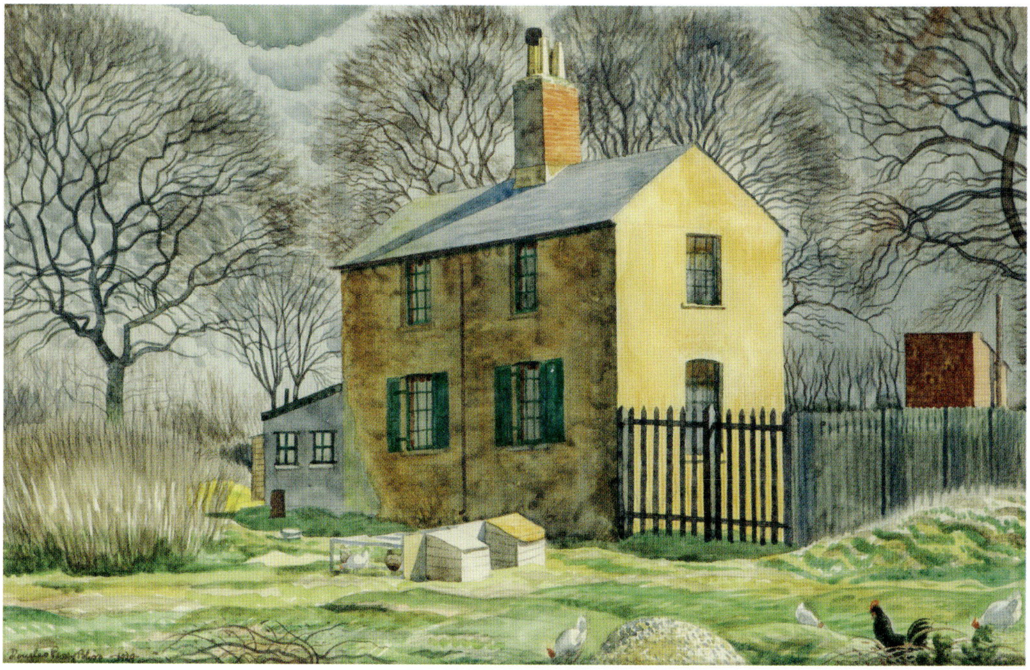

Douglas Percy Bliss (1900-1984)

Cottage with picket fence, 1929

Signed and dated, watercolour - 31 x 47 cm.

This watercolour is very similar in spirit to those featured in Bliss's first ever exhibition - a joint show with his friends and fellow Royal College of Art students, Eric Ravilious and Edward Bawden, held at the St George's Gallery in Hanover Square,1927. In *Gargoyles & Tattie-Bogles*, The Fleece Press, 2017, Malcolm Yorke summed up this nascent moment in the lives of these three young artists as follows: 'Bawden was the weakest of the three in terms of landscape painting and he further handicapped himself by using unsuitable non-absorbent paper. Ravilious too was still tentatively exploring that dry handling of subdued tones which characterised his mature works. Douglas, on the other hand, showed watercolours which were already assured and colourful...' When critics accused Bliss of merely aping, his mentor, Paul Nash with 'mild and mannered modernity' he was irritated, feeling that his own work had more to do with the British tradition of watercolour painting, exemplified by Palmer, Cotman, Towne and Rowlandson. Bliss held such work to be amongst 'England's most characteristic and valuable contribution to the art of the world'.

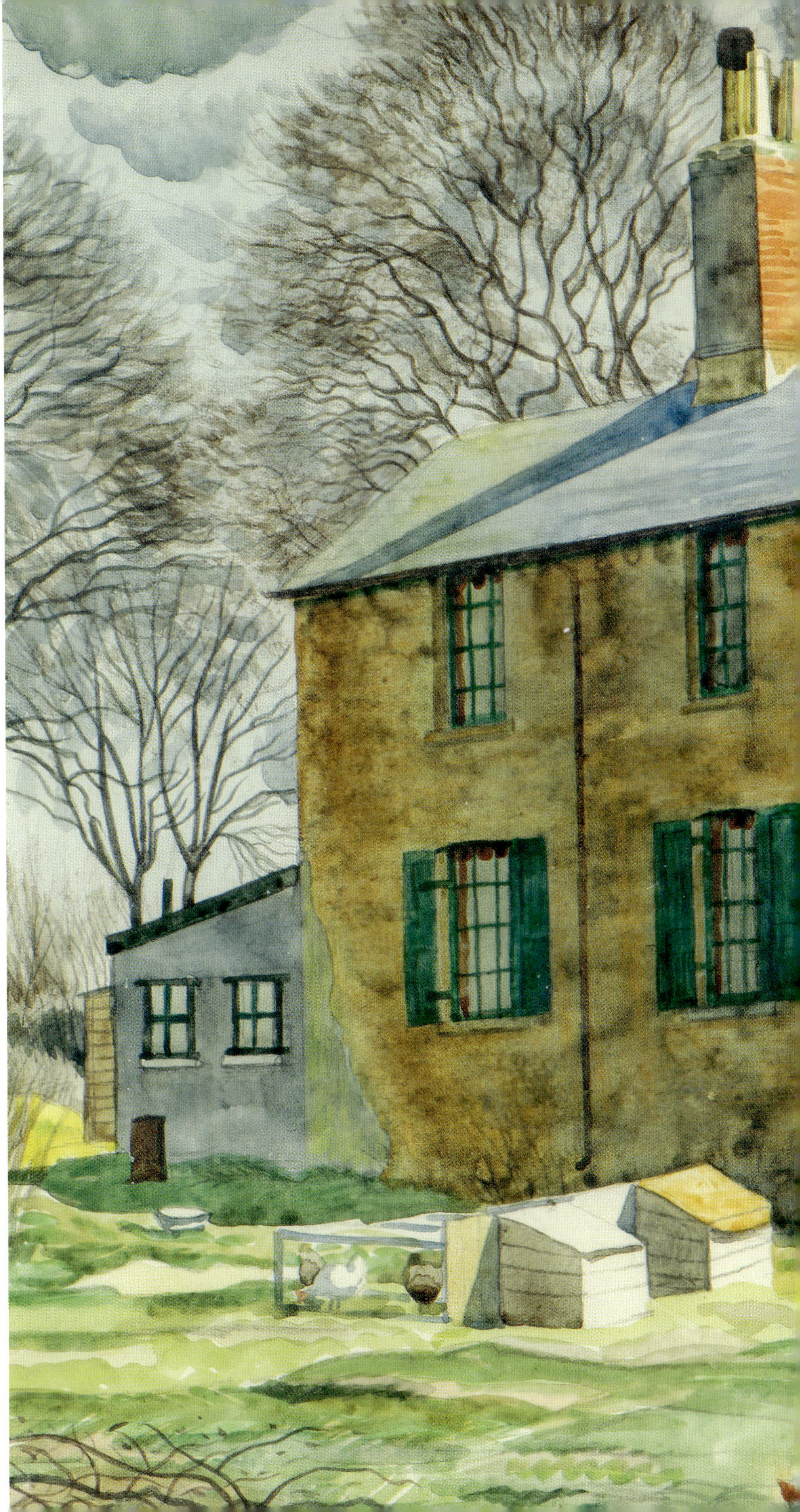

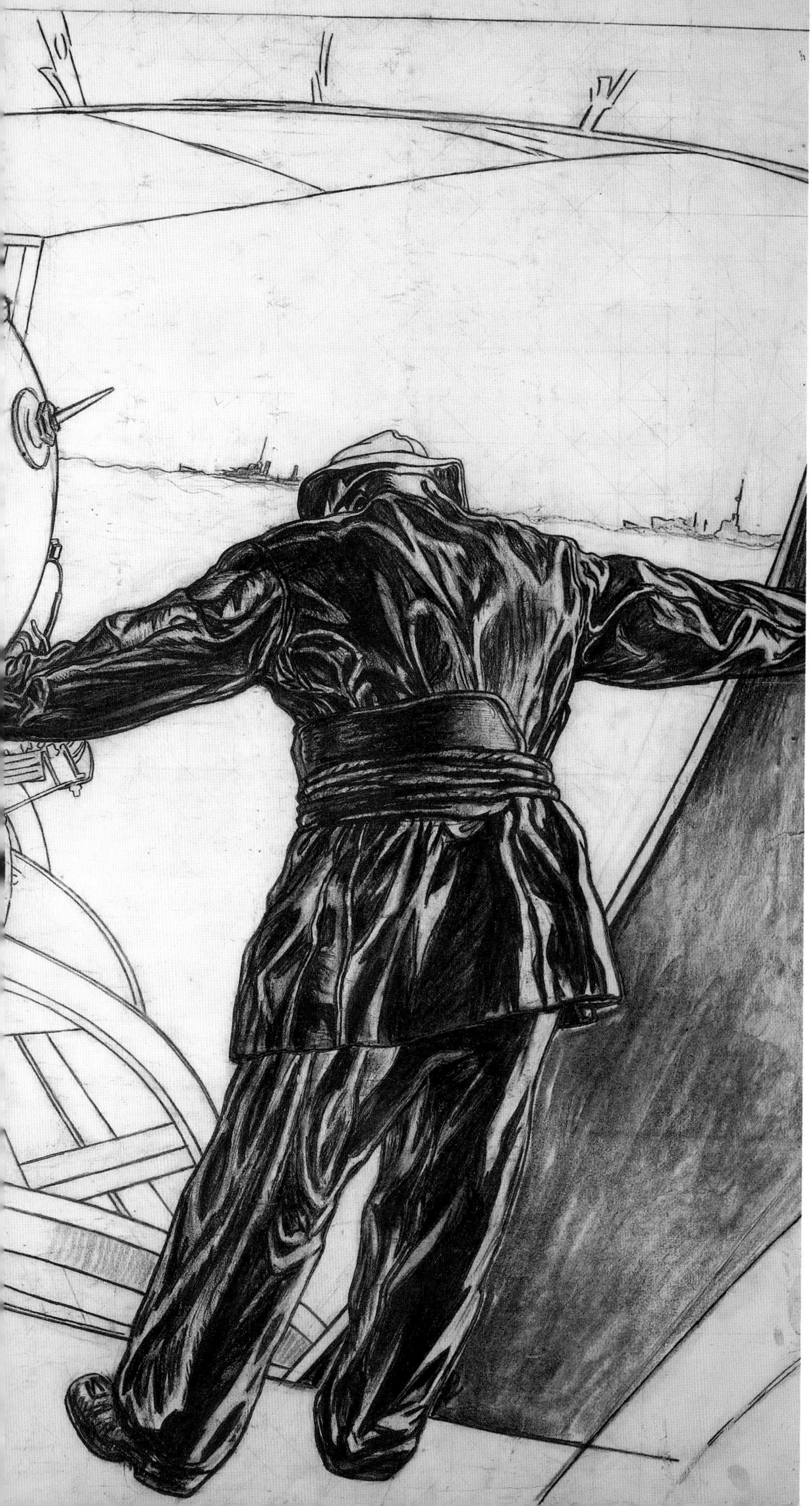

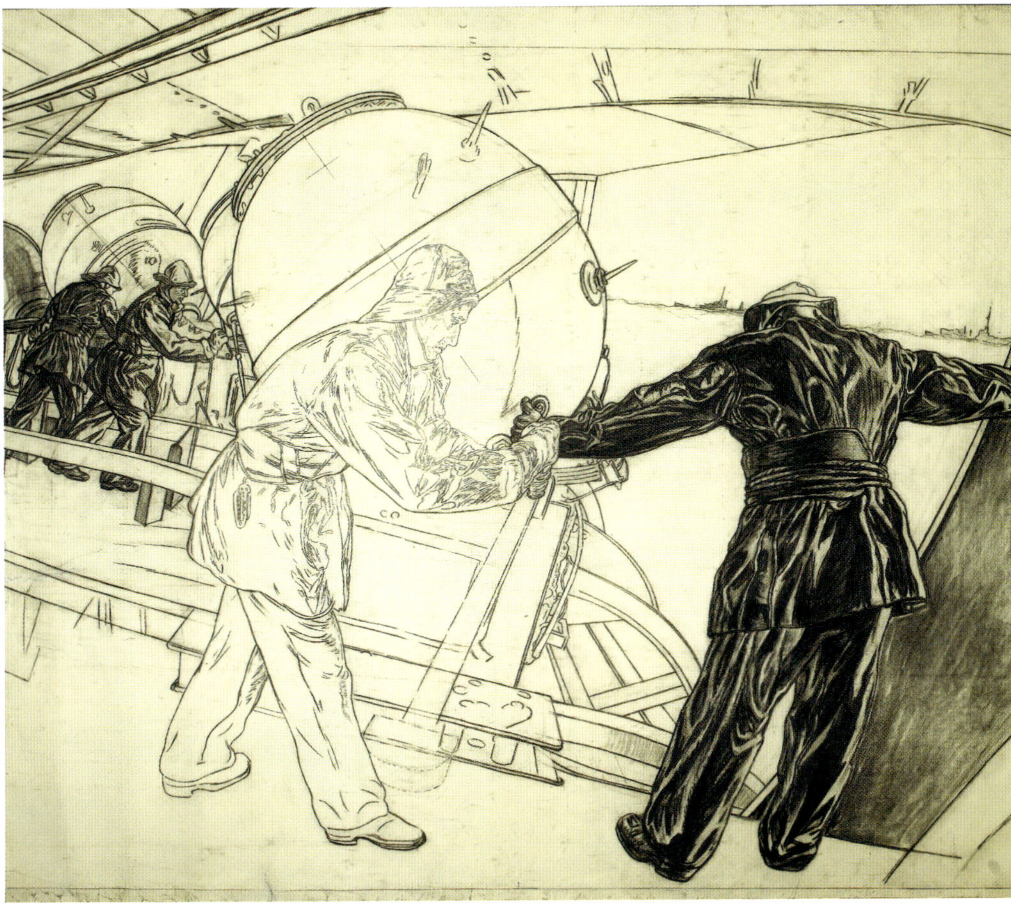

Muirhead Bone (1876-1953)

Full size drawing for Winter Mine-Laying off Iceland, circa 1942

Charcoal - 127.9 x 160.6 cm.

Muirhead Bone served as an Official War Artist during both WW1 and WW2. Numerous studies of minesweepers in action, culminating in this vigorous full-sized cartoon, resulted in one of his most ambitious wartime paintings: Winter Mine-Laying off Iceland, 1942, (collection IWM). *The Diaries of Randolph Schwabe* (edited by Gill Clarke published by Sansom & Co. 2016), record that Bone invited Schwarbe to tea 'to look at the progress of his picture of the mine -layer: .... big drawings of the men laying the mines ... very secret and unpublishable... which I ought not to have seen: all done at sea, under very difficult conditions, with obstacles that only Bone could surmount.'

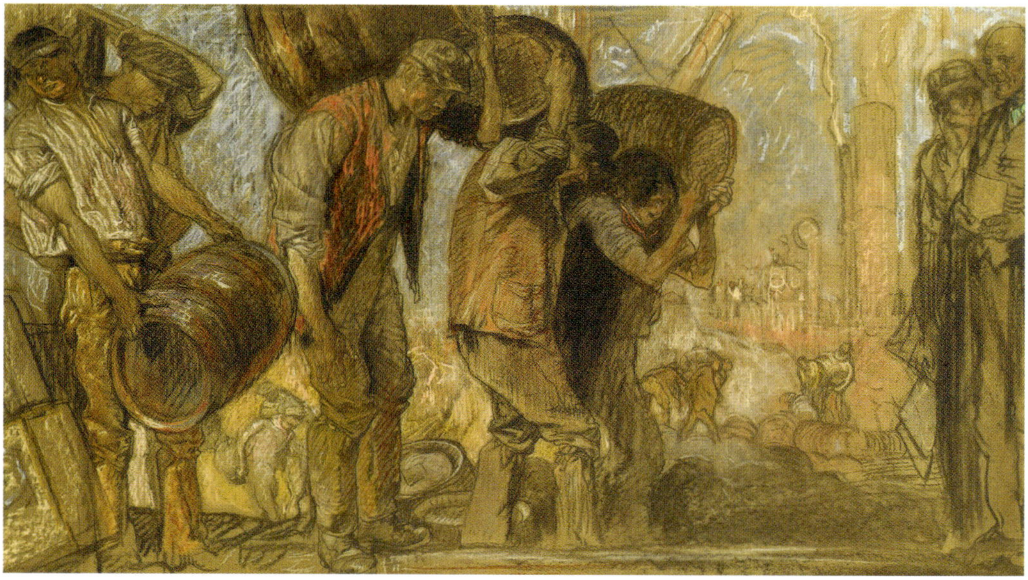

Frank Brangwyn (1867-1956)

Study for Beer Porters, Lloyd's Register of Shipping, circa 1910

Charcoal and chalk, squared - 73 x 120 cm.

The Committee Luncheon Room, for Lloyd's Register of Shipping, Fenchurch Street, London was decorated by Brangwyn from 1908-1914. The scheme comprised eleven paintings in tempera on canvas: four panels measuring 137.2x121.9cm (4ft 6inx4ft), four panels measuring 137.2x243.8cm (4ft 6inx8ft), two panels measuring 137.2x91.4cm (4ft 6inx3ft) and a lunette which measured 243.8x670.6cm (8x22ft). The commission was gained through Sir Thomas Lane Devitt, then Chairman of Lloyd's Register of Shipping. The panels, illustrating porters in the London docks, were removed in the late 1960s, stored and subsequently lost.

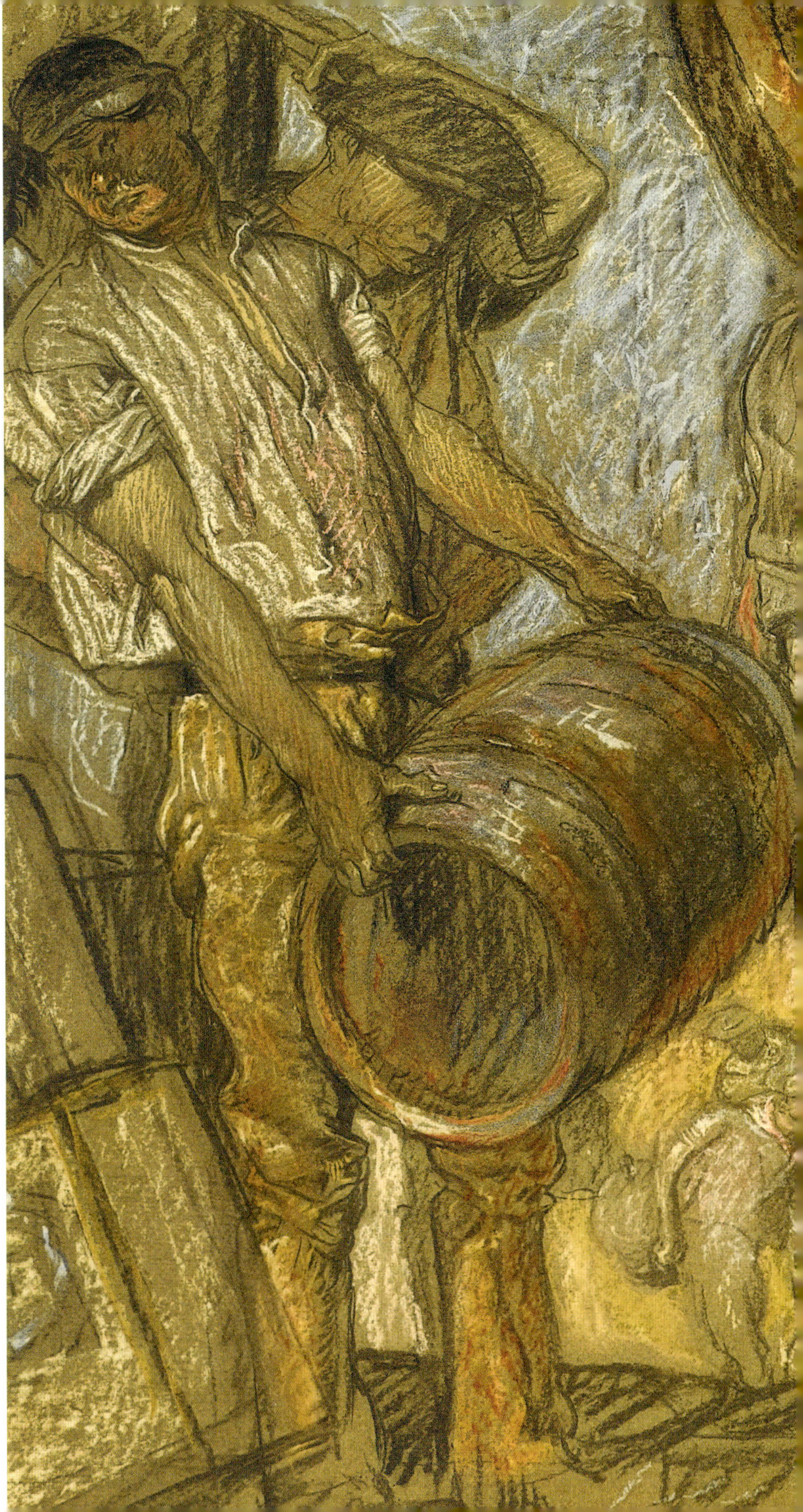

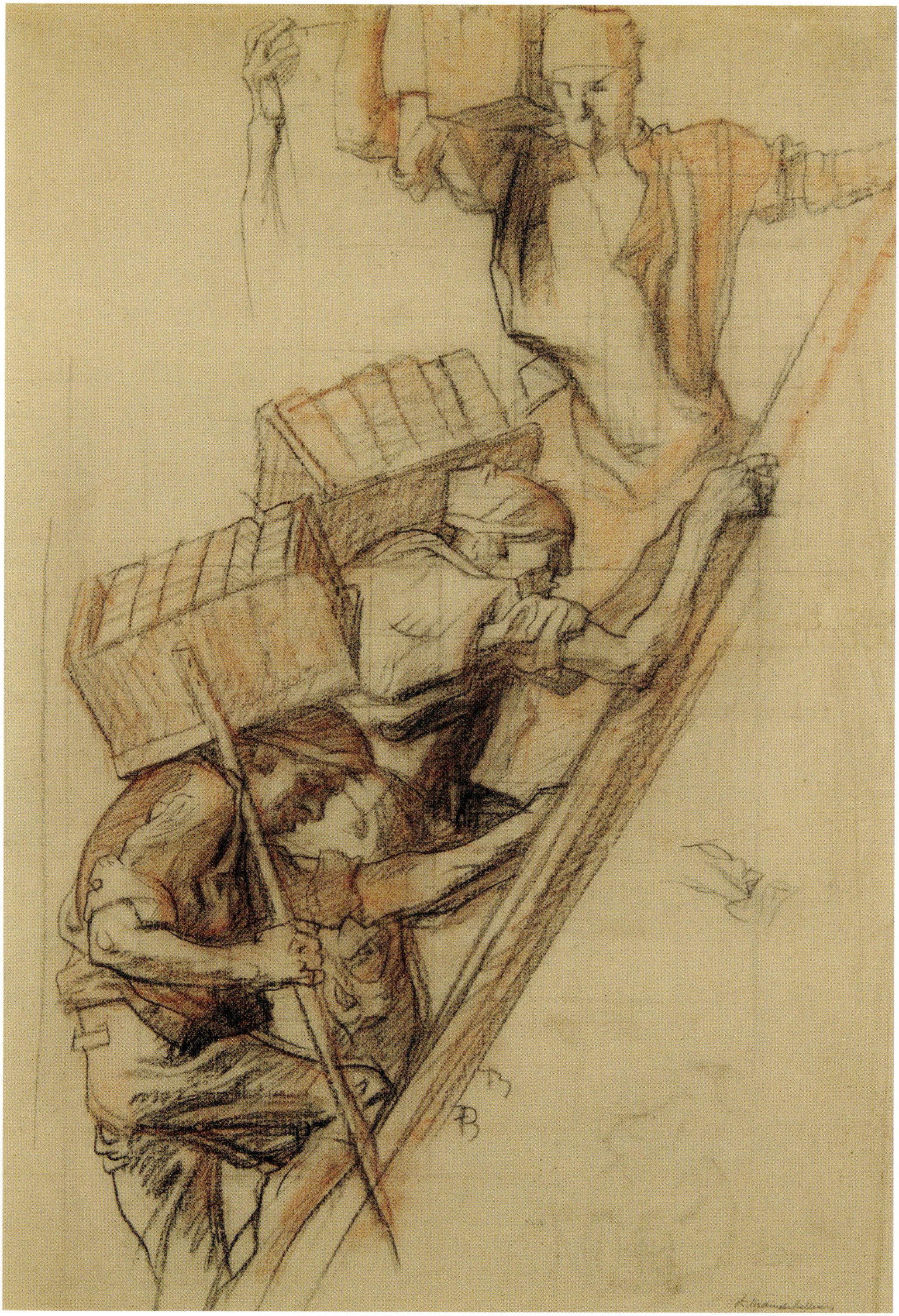

Frank Brangwyn (1867-1956)

Bricklayers, a study for Rebuilding Belgium, 1915

Signed with monogram (twice), black and red chalk on buff paper, squared - 69 x 47 cm.

Brangwyn was one of the most prolific draftsmen of his generation. While his near contemporaries Augustus John (1878-1961) and William Orpen (1878-1931) arguably had greater technical facility, Brangwyn's vigorous approach to drawing and directness of observation place him amongst the greatest draughtsmen of 20th century art. As the art critic T. W. Earp stated, 'It is in the drawings... that the key to Brangwyn's greatness is to be found'.

This drawing is a study for a poster designed by Brangwyn entitled 'The Remaking of Belgium', issued as an auto lithograph. The exhibition took place at University College London, in 1915, to help Belgians to prepare for reconstruction after the War.

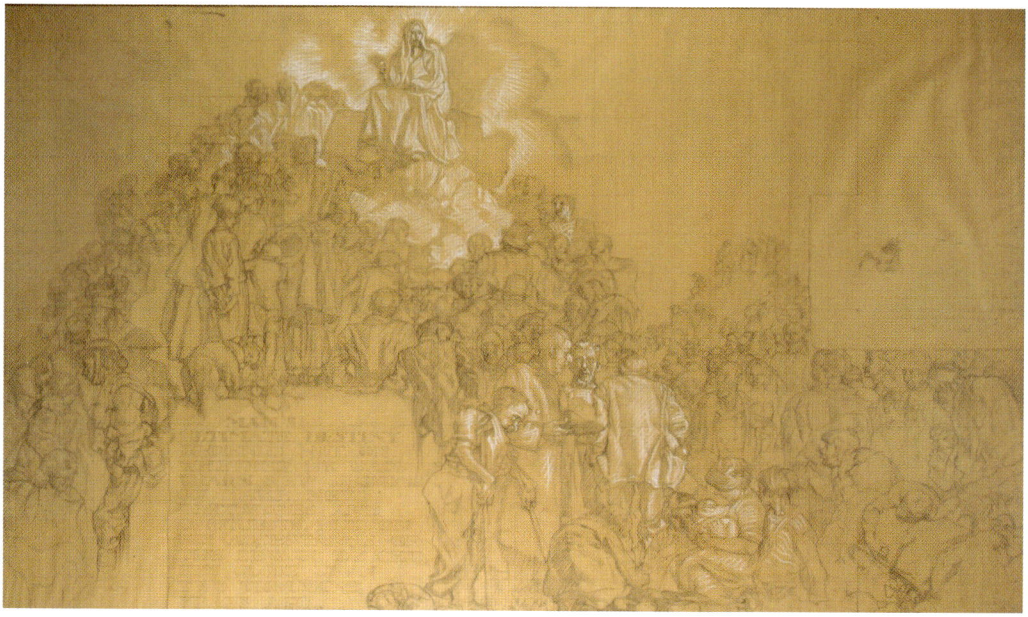

Frank Brangwyn (1867-1956)

Study for Man's Ultimate Destiny, circa 1932

Pencil on buff coloured tracing paper, squared, with highlights in white chalk
152.4 x 213.4 cm.

Brangwyn's murals for the Rockefeller Center, New York, adorn the lifts in the main atrium. The mural scheme gained notoriety when Diego Rivera's contribution - *Man at the Crossroads* - was controversially painted over after Rivera refused Rockefeller's request that he remove a portrait of Lenin from the composition. Like Rivera, Brangwyn also had to navigate requests for alterations ; but by nature he was less keen to court controversy. This cartoon shows Brangwyn's original proposal in which Christ is seen seated on a hill facing the viewer. In the final design after the intervention of Rockefeller, who wished for there to be no religious figures included, Brangwyn simply turned the figure of Christ round ; the joke being that Christ had turned his back on Rockefeller. The area to the left of the lettering was also eliminated in the final work.

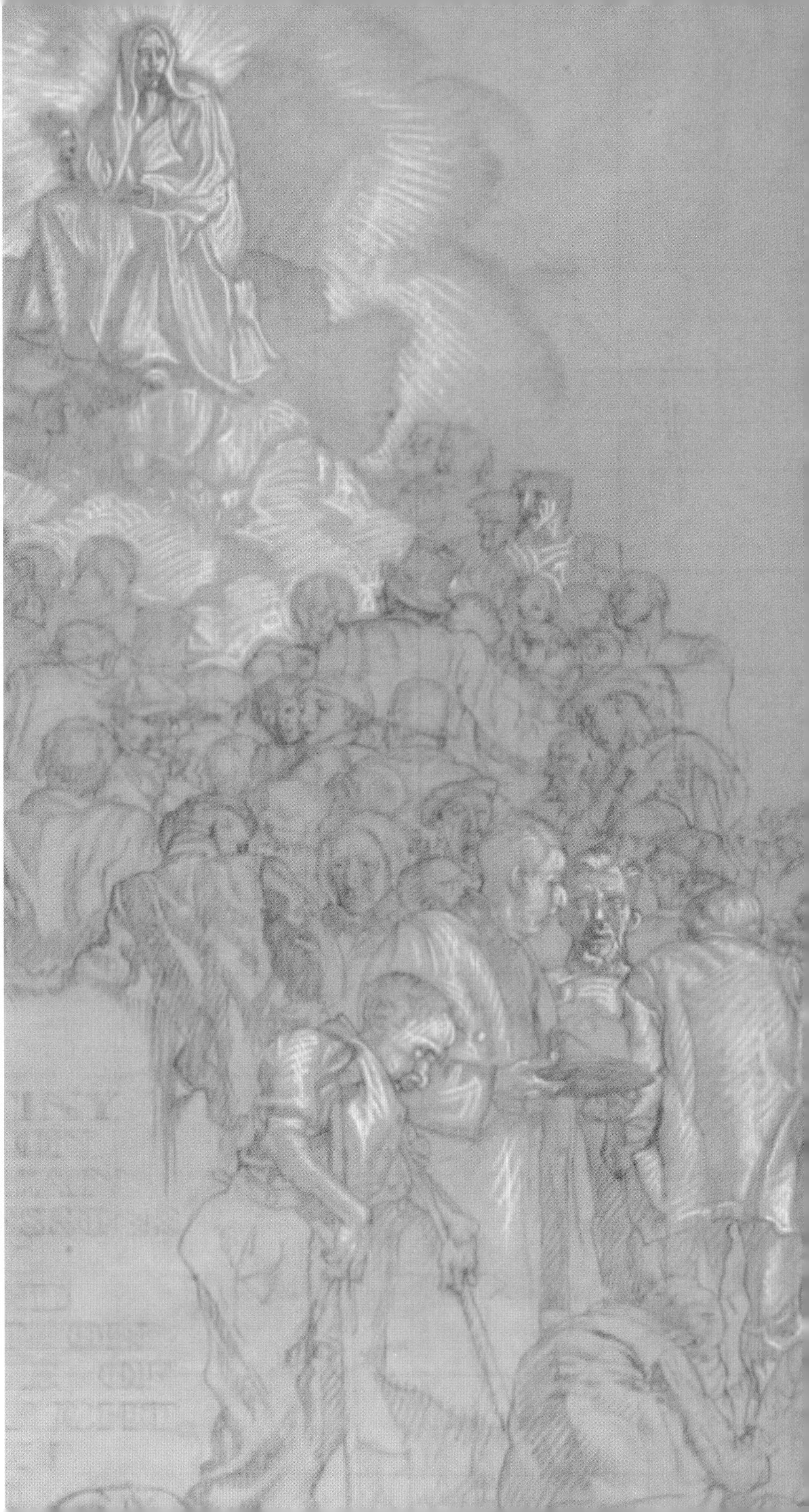

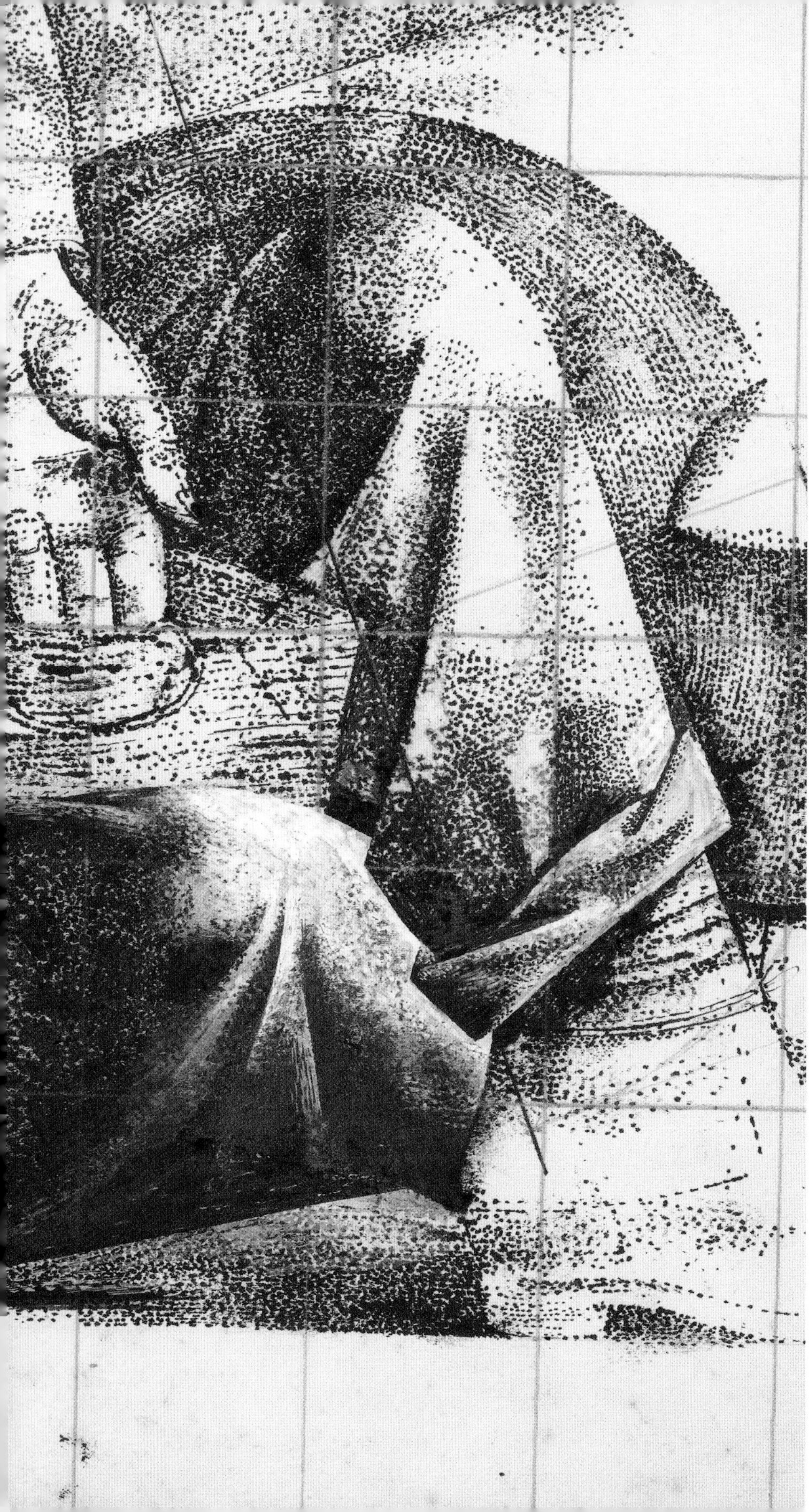

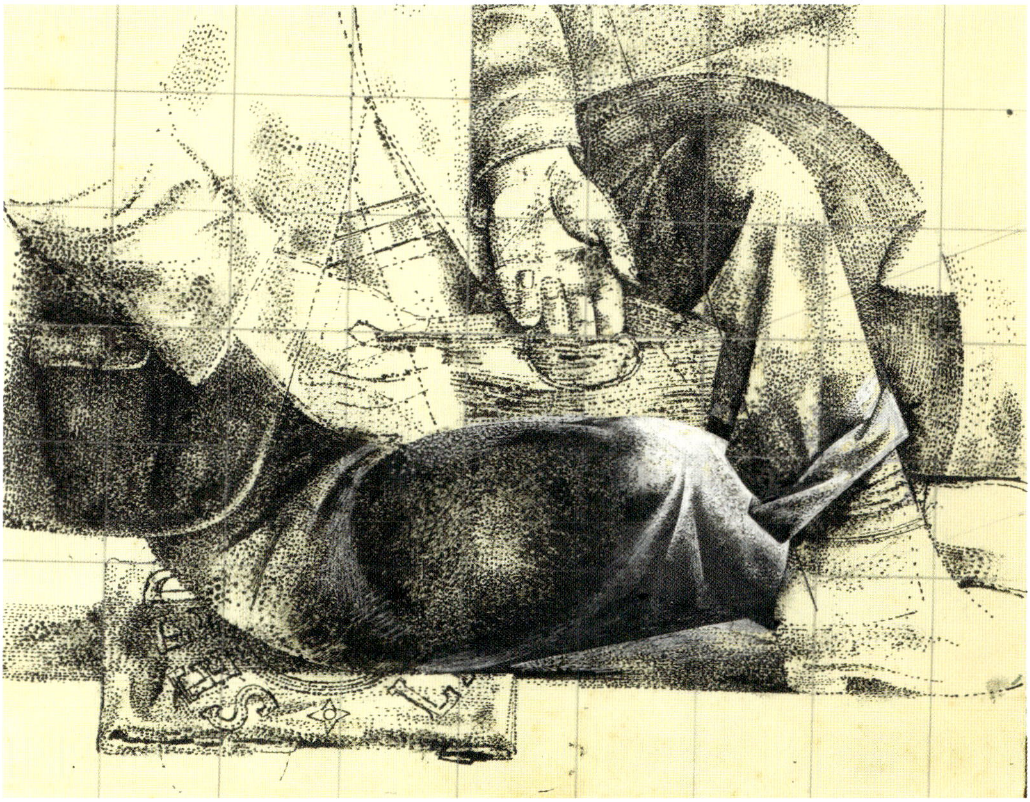

Reginald Brill (1902-1974)

Study for The Rest, 1956

Pen and ink with white highlights, squared - 32 x38 cm.

This study is for one of Brill's most celebrated paintings from his series 'Martyrdom of Man' – a group of ambitious oils that sought to elevate the everyday lives of figures usually taken for granted by society. To add pathos 'The Rest' recalls Piero della Francesca's Resurrection. As the winner of the Rome Scholarship in Decorative Painting for 1927 Brill developed both a high distinctive pointilliste drawing technique combined with a deep appreciation of Renaissance art and the traditional manner of crafting compositions through a series of highly worked, and at times pattern-book style, preparatory drawings, where favourite studies are available to be reused again and again.

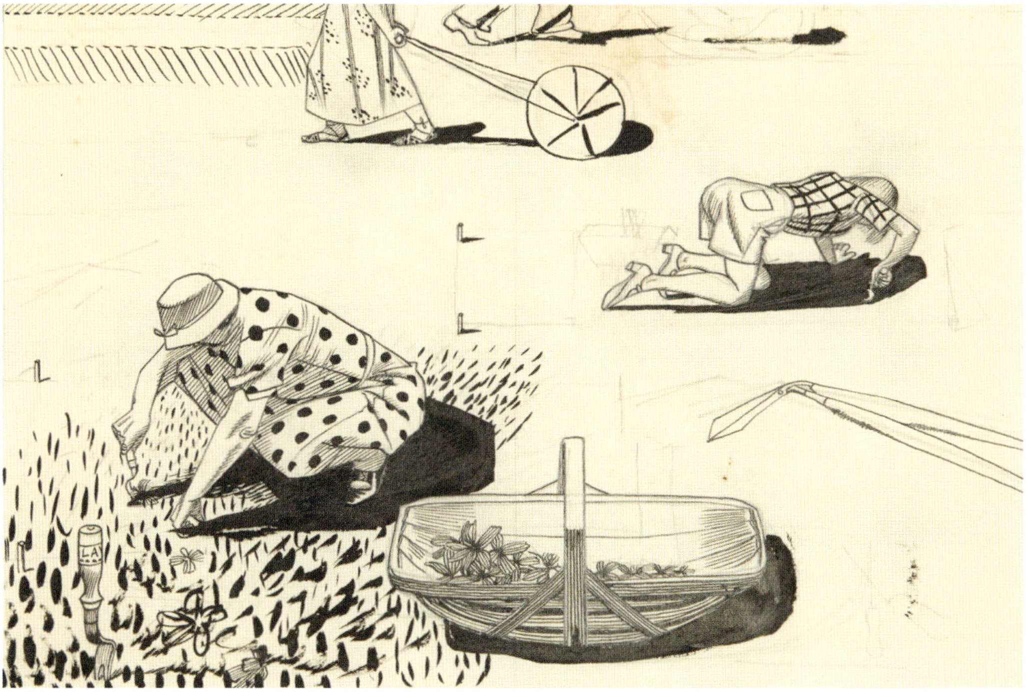

Evelyn Dunbar (1906-1960)

Studies for vignettes for Country Life, Gardener's Diary, 1938

Pen and ink, pencil - 38 x 57 cm.

Noel Carrington, Dunbar's Hampstead landlord, was keen to promote the work of those artists he admired. In 1937 as editor at Country Life Ltd he commissioned Ravilious to illustrate '*The Country Life Cookery Book*' and Edward Bawden '*The Gardener's Diary*'. These were followed in 1938 by the now celebrated '*High Street*', again illustrated by Ravilious, and a further '*Gardener's Diary*' illustrated by Evelyn Dunbar. Each month was illustrated by its personification - some were later worked up into oils - while depictions of gardeners, male and female, and their activities served as vignettes and tailpieces. Dunbar took the opportunity through a studied awkwardness to emphasise the fact that physical labour is the gardener's lot throughout the year.

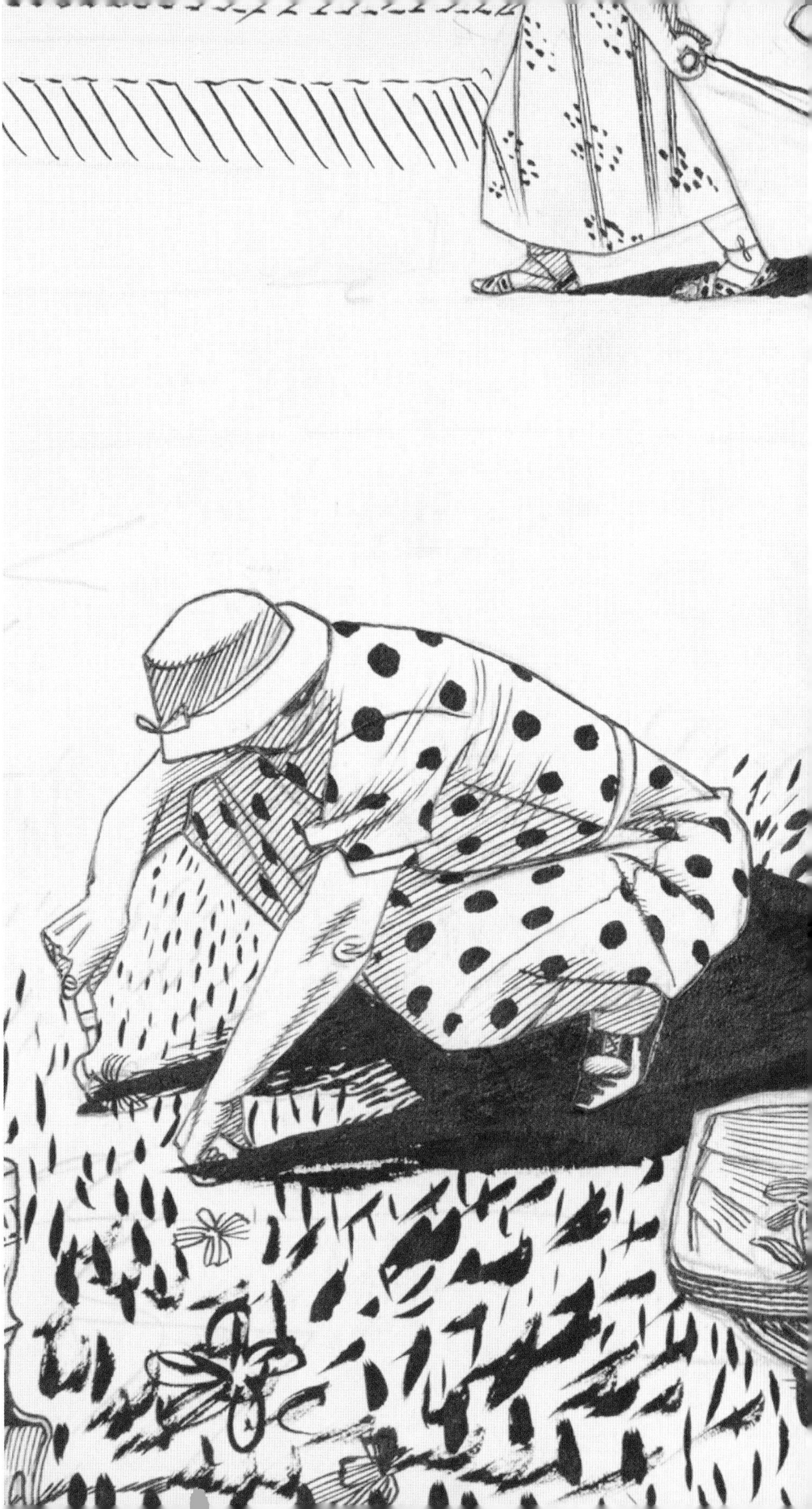

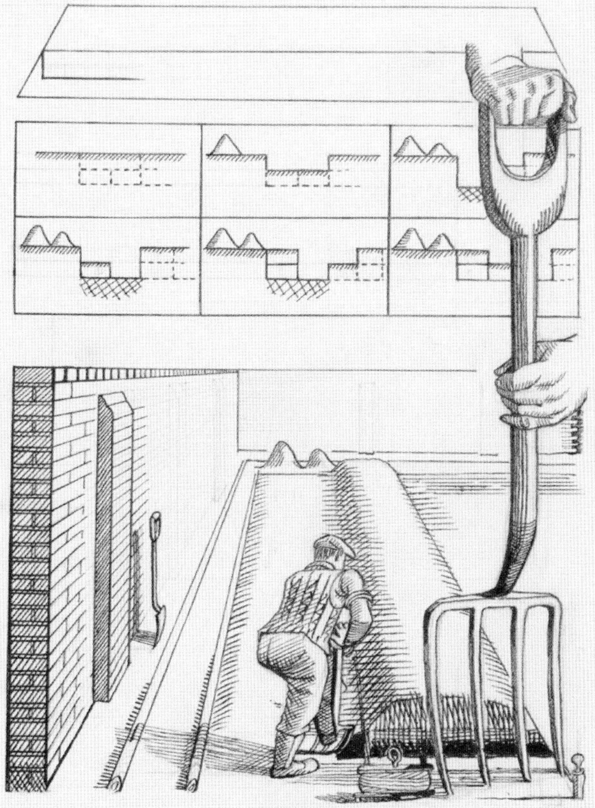

Evelyn Dunbar (1906-1960)

A diagrammatic explanation of trenching or double digging, circa 1937

Pen and ink - 25.3 x 20.2 cm.

This diagrammatic explanation of trenching was prepared for an unidentified gardening manual. The buttressed garden wall can be associated with the wall at The Cedars, the Dunbar family home in Strood, Rochester. The design is reminiscent of vignettes for *Gardeners' Choice* (Routledge, 1937: Persephone Books, 2015) jointly written and illustrated with Charles Mahoney.

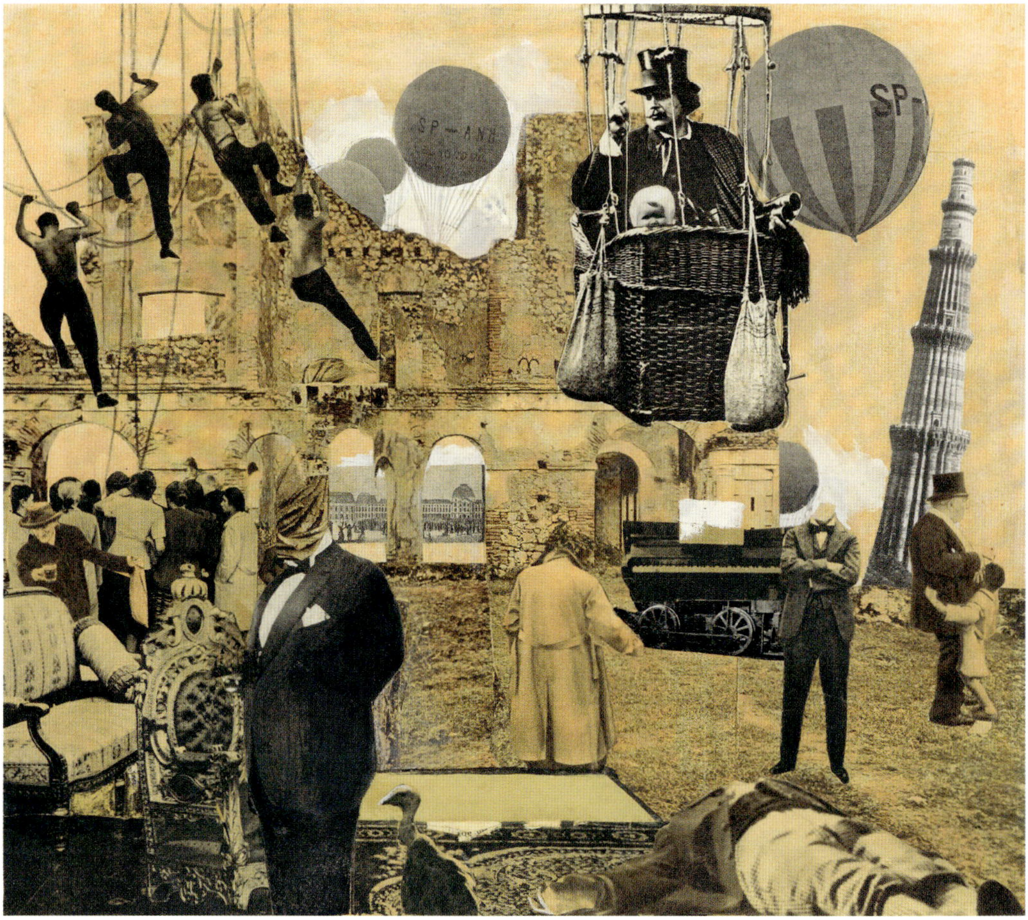

David Evans, (1929-1988)

Up in the Air, circa 1960

Collage including pencil, watercolour, gouache and photomontage - 32 x 35 cm.

Early in his career Evans showed photo-montages at fashionable London restaurants such as Gallery One and gained several commissions. These included a design for the Hollywood Room in the Observer Film Exhibition, 1956, and a mural for the Soup Kitchen, Knightsbridge. Until recently Evans early work remained unrecorded - its rediscovery allows for a fuller understanding of his development as an artist.

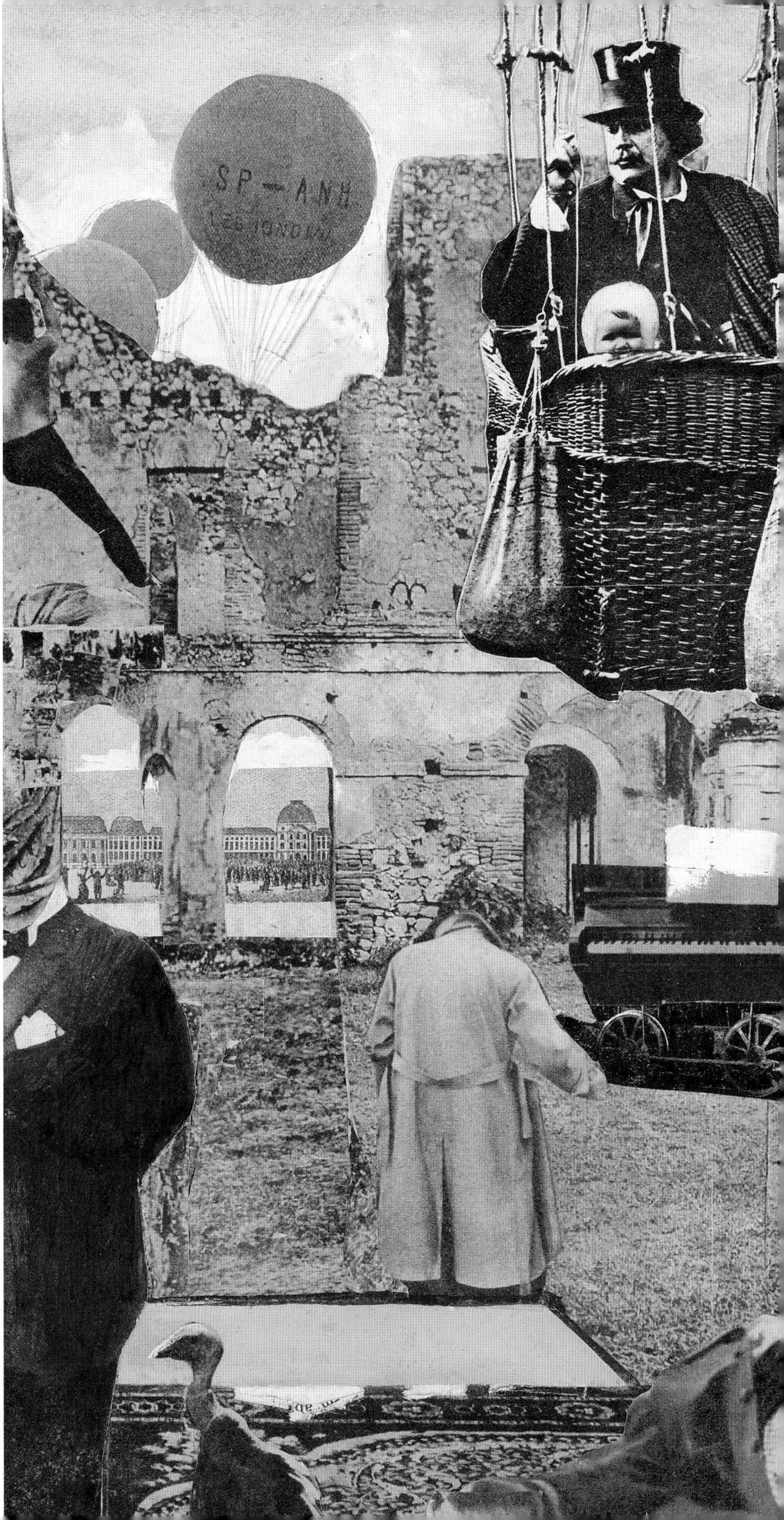
SP — ANH

Hubert Arthur Finney (1905-1991)

The Old Stove, late 30's

Pencil and pastel - 53.3 x 39.4 cm.

This composition bears witness to Finney's desire to observe and elevate everyday objects. In his unpublished memoir Finney spoke of his 'passion for drawing', and his 'continuous sense of awakening to the beauty found in even the dreariest of surroundings', and through which his 'yearnings to create were increased not diminished'. Prolific by nature, sadly most of his pre-WW2 work was destroyed when his Chiswick studio was hit by a bomb during WW2. 'One my great regret is that I did not preserve or try to keep some of the drawings and paintings that I made during these formative years, when one's vision was fresh and one's emotional response to things was intense and full of excitement...'

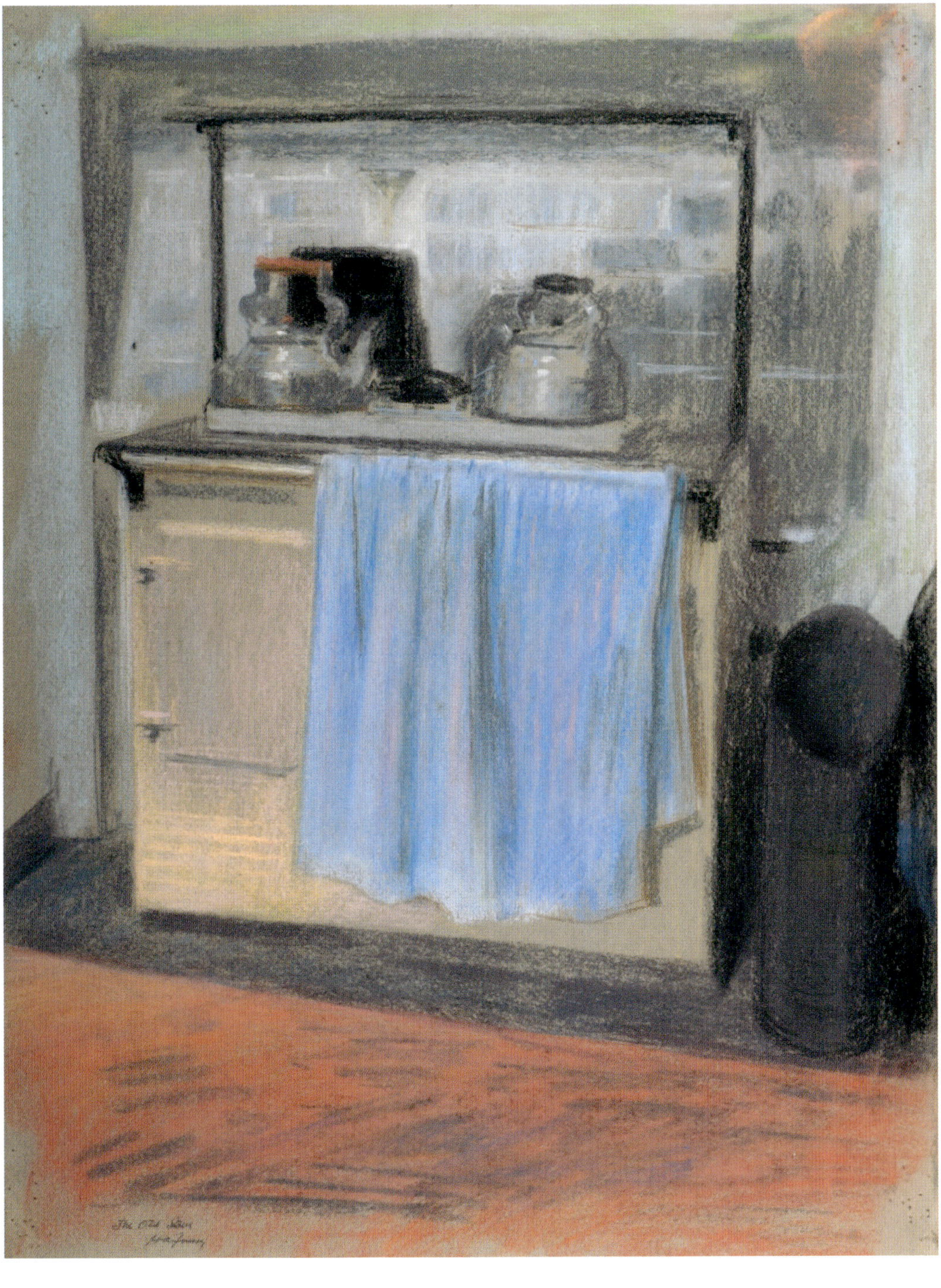

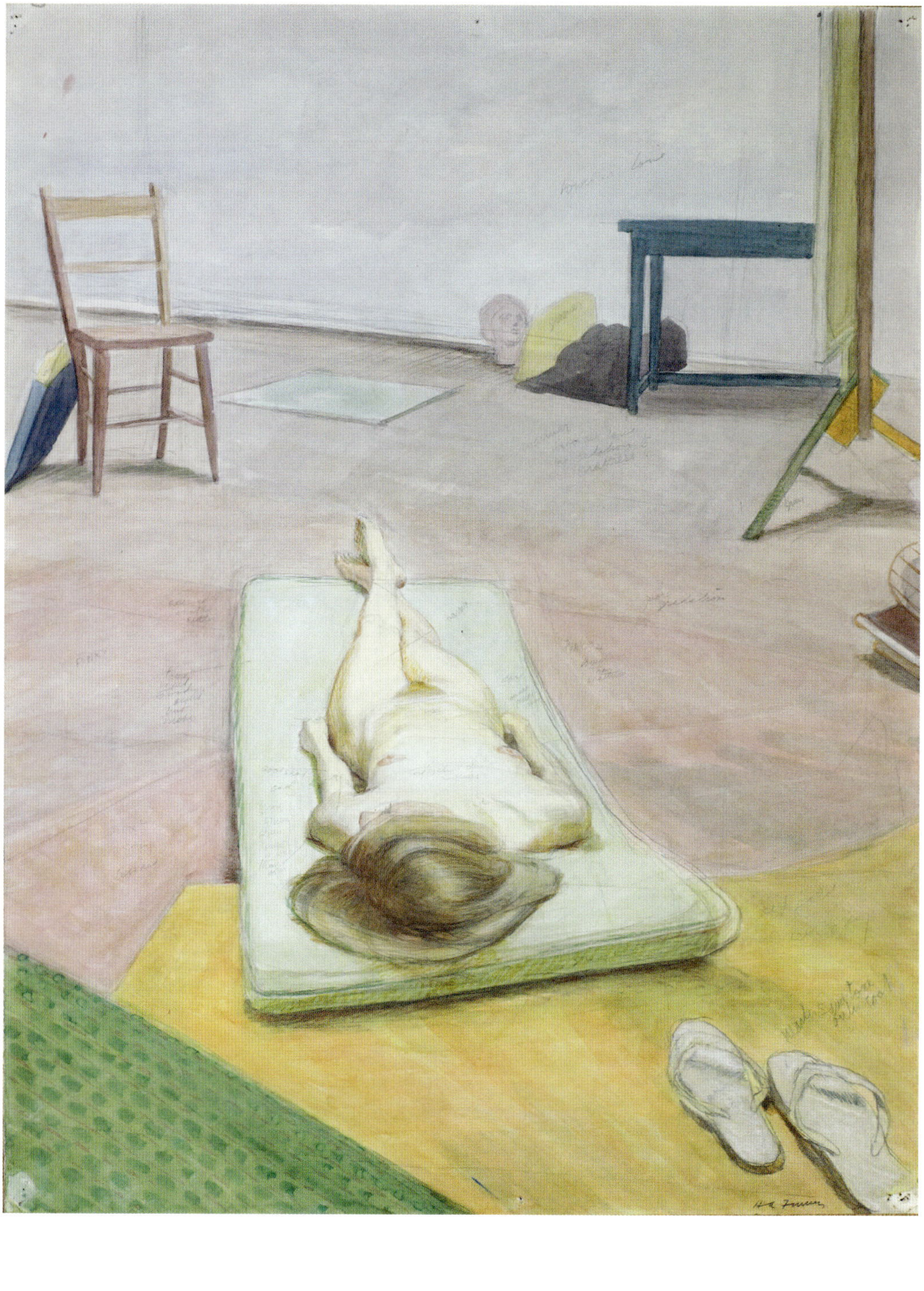

Hubert Arthur Finney (1905-1991)

The Artist's Model in the Studio, circa 1930

Watercolour - 50.8 x 38.1 cm.

This study dates to the 1930's when Finney taught at Chelsea School of Art, alongside Henry Moore, who was in charge of the Sculpture Department, and Graham Sutherland, who was in charge of the Design Department. From the end of WW2 until his retirement in 1970 Finney was in charge of Life Drawing at Reading University.

'Art' Finney remarked, 'enables us to have an awareness of beauty in the world, and a greater sensitivity to people which leads us to a richer appreciation of life. I was involuntarily directed toward the human head and figure. I have an inborn sense of tonal relationships and even now after sixty years not much of the pleasure of painting is inseparable from beauty of tone...'

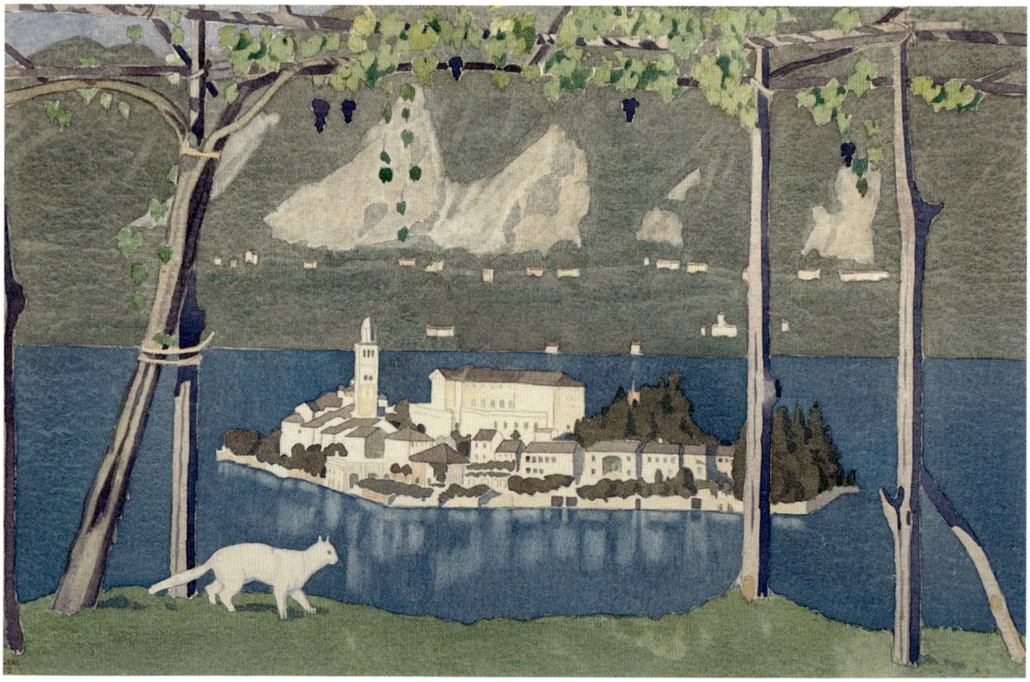

Margaret Gere (1878-1965)

The White Cat, Isola San Giulio, Lake Orta, 1928

Signed, titled and dated, watercolour over drawing - 25 x 38 cm.

A founder member of the Birmingham Group of Artists-Craftsmen and a noted tempera artist, Gere made several study trips to Italy, often in the company of her half-brother the artist Charles Gere with whom she lived in Painswick, Gloucestershire. They were among the earliest members of the Cheltenham Group. This work was in the collection of Charles H St. John Hornby (1867-1946), founder of the Ashendene Press. Isola di San Giulio is an island in Lake Orta, Piedmont.

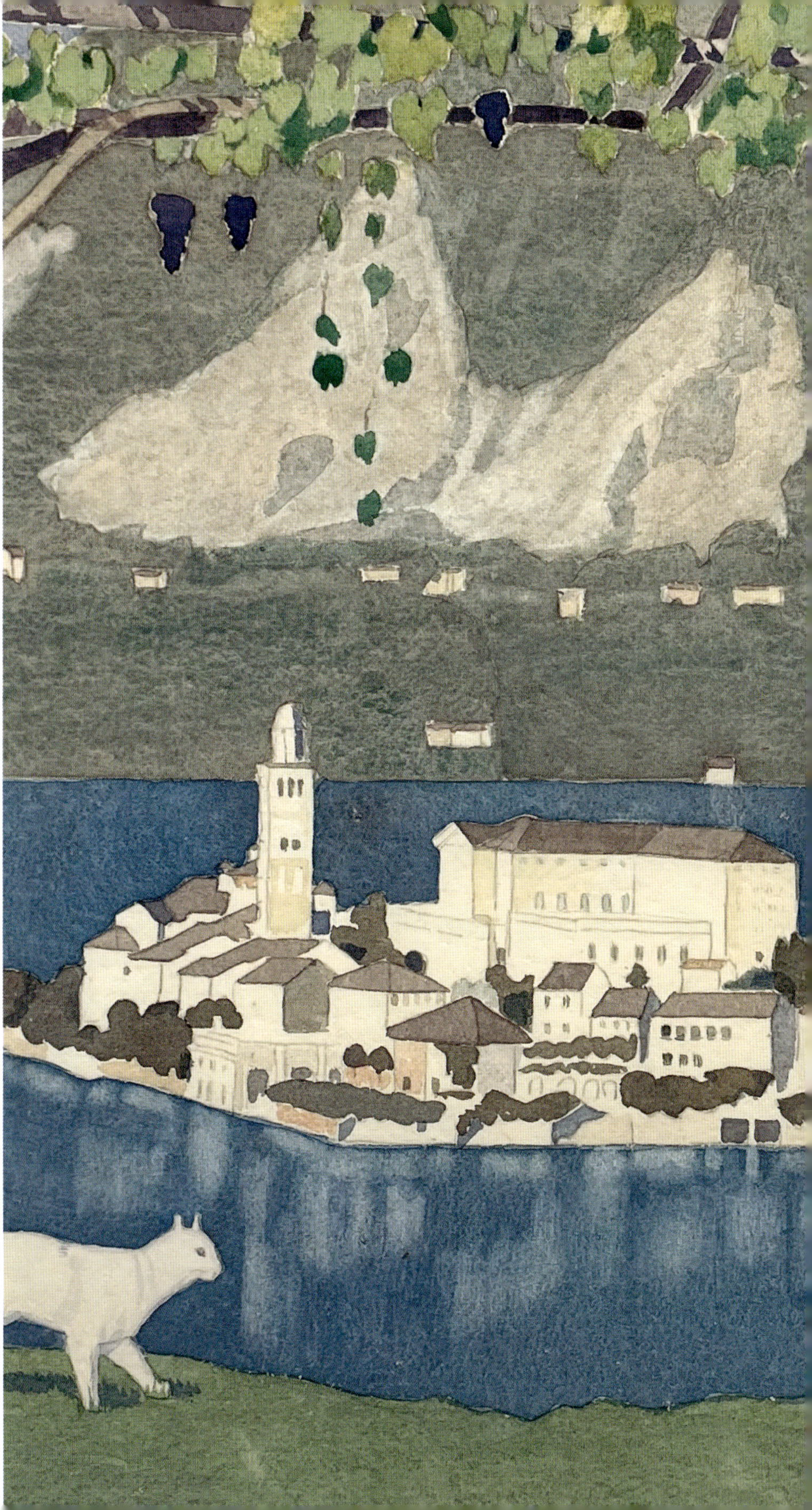

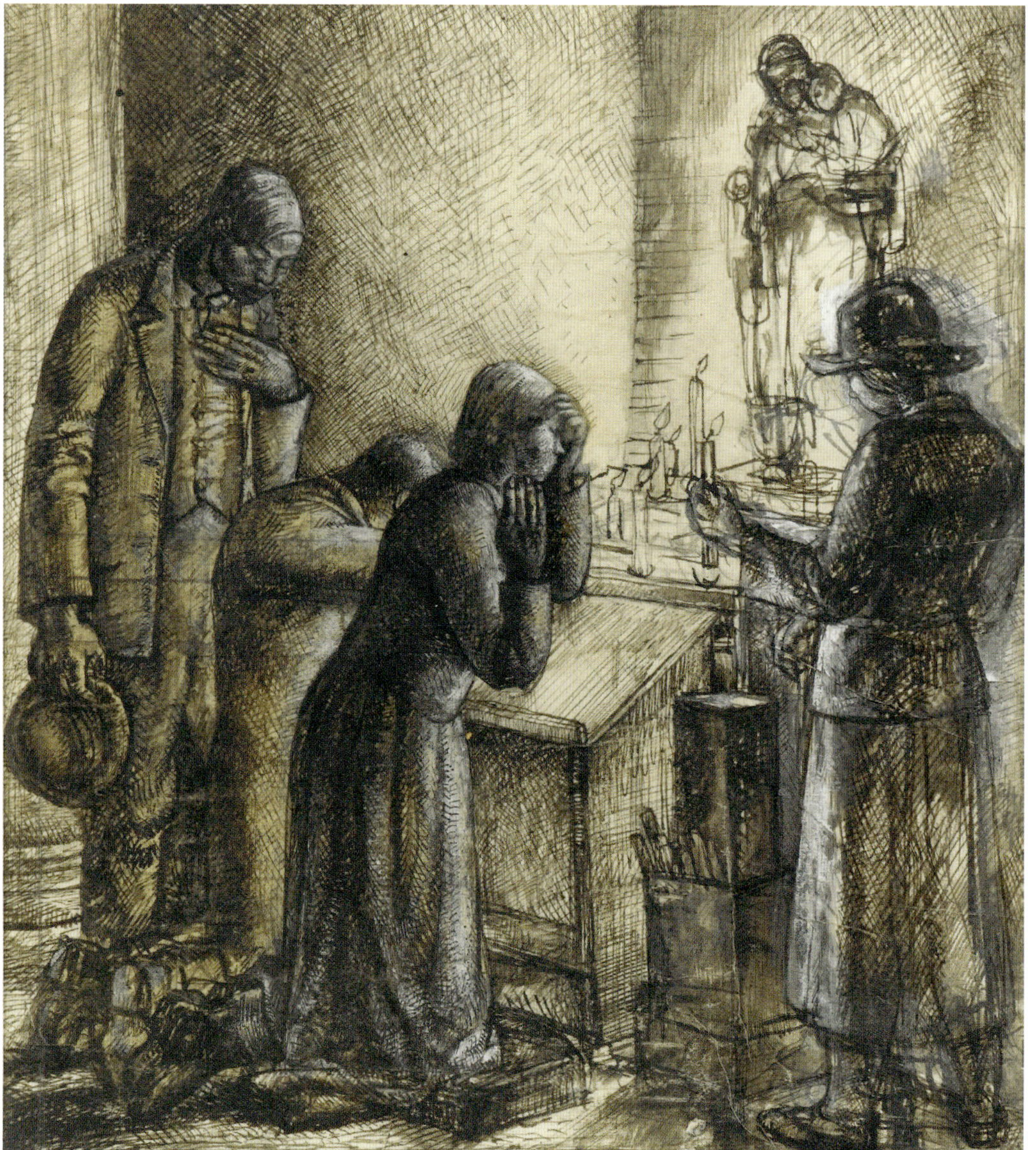

Evelyn Gibbs (1905-1991)

The Chapel, 1928

Pen and ink with white highlights - 14.8 x 13.2 cm.

Evelyn Gibbs trained as a graphic artist and more particularly as a printmaker in etching and engraving, winning a scholarship to the Royal College of Art in 1926 and from there a further scholarship to the British School at Rome in 1929, The Chapel was based on studies made in Westminster Cathedral. Gibbs uses emphatic hatching and cross-hatching to intensify the religious and emotional atmosphere, each intended mark visible in this original drawing, ready for transfer, in reverse, to the copper plate.

Edith Granger-Taylor (1887-1958)

Three Figures, circa 1910

Signed with monogram, oil over pencil on panel - 36 x 26 cm.

This panel, with its sinuous asymmetrical design typical of the prevalent Art Nouveau style of the period, dates to Edith Granger-Taylor's student years at the Royal Academy. According to the artist's grandson, the artist Nicolas Granger-Taylor, 'in her oil studies of this period she was beginning to emphasize an aspect of colour and shape, and of pattern, that would come to define her later, more modern and often near-abstract style.'

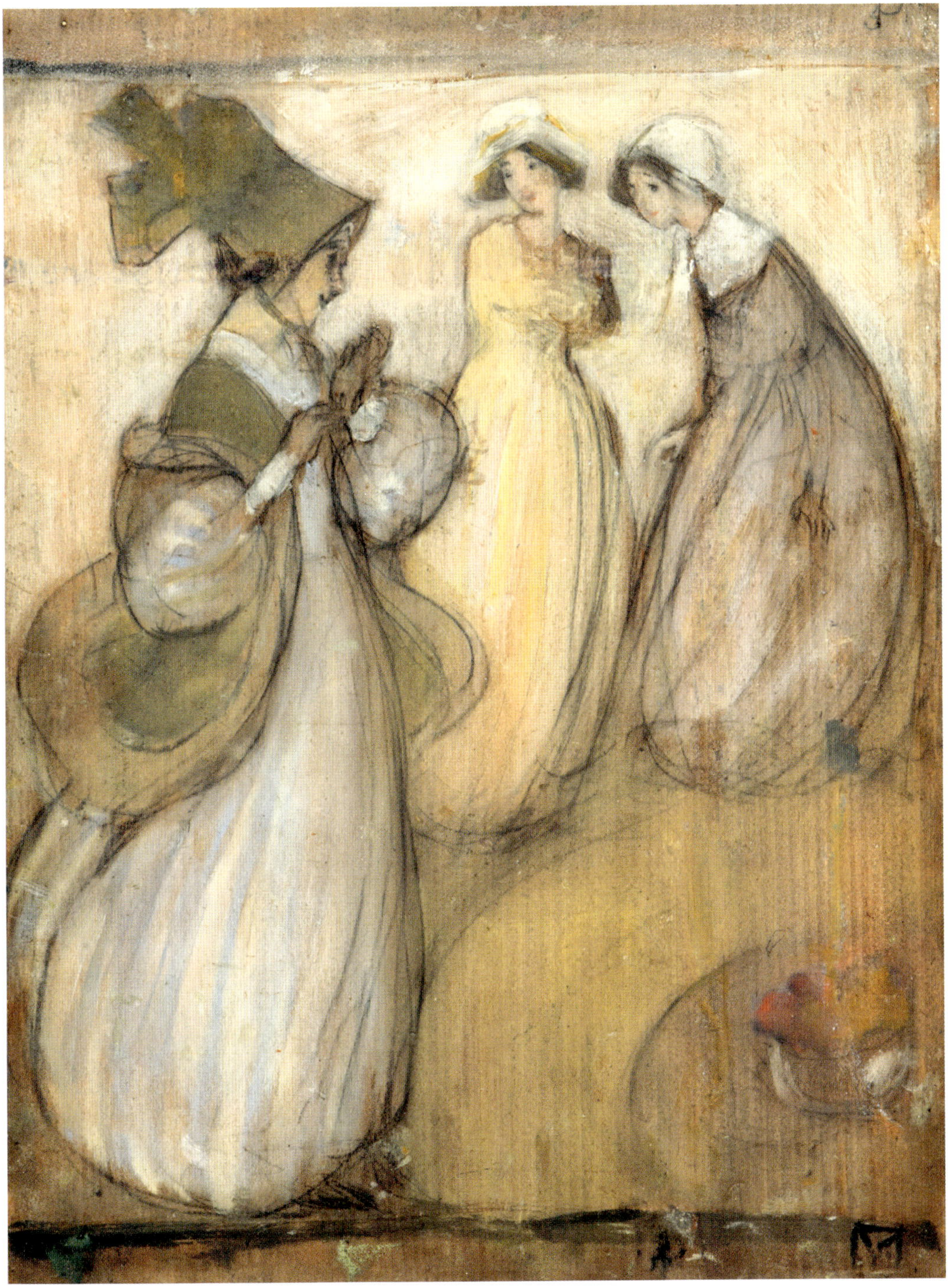

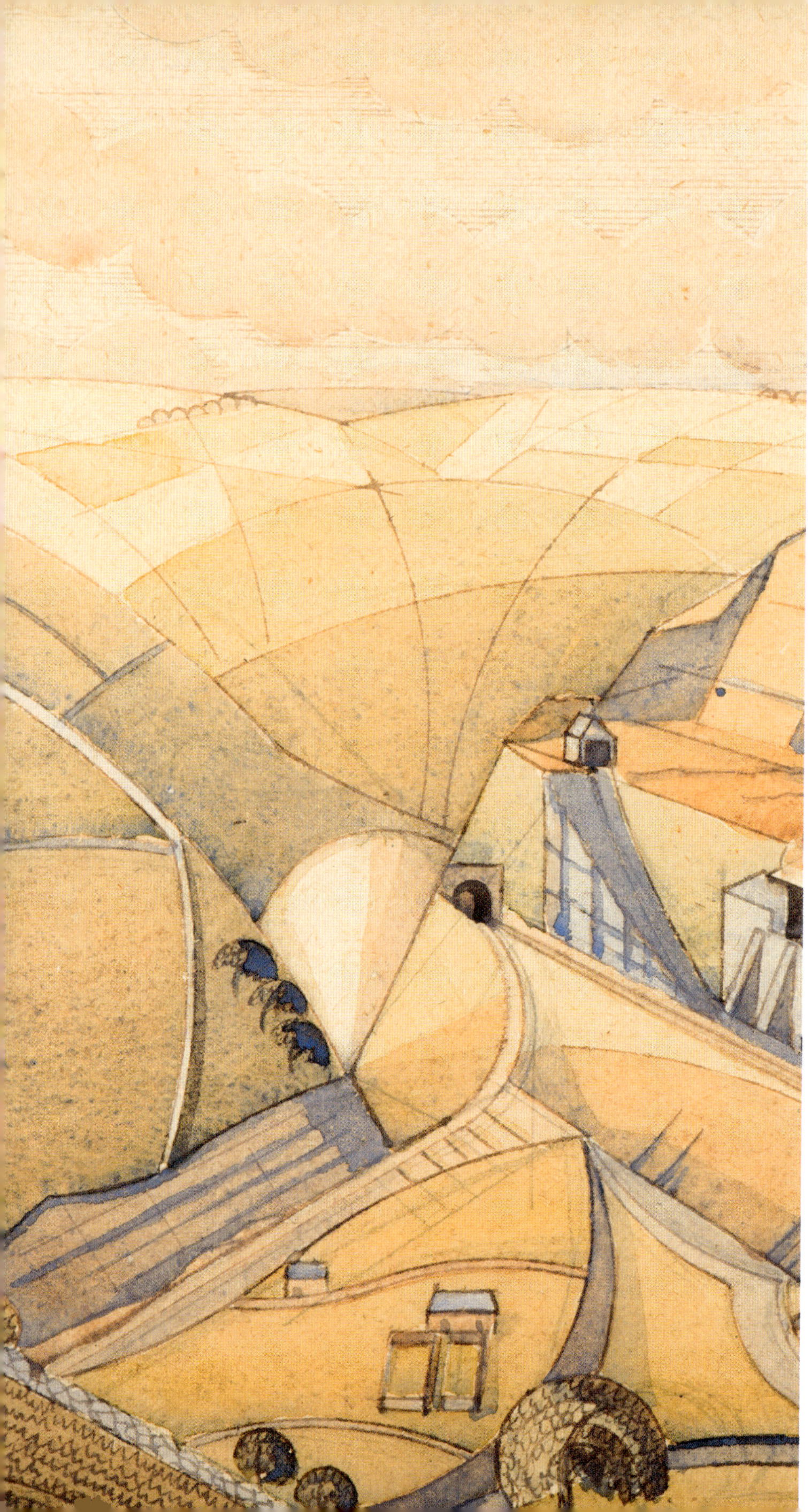

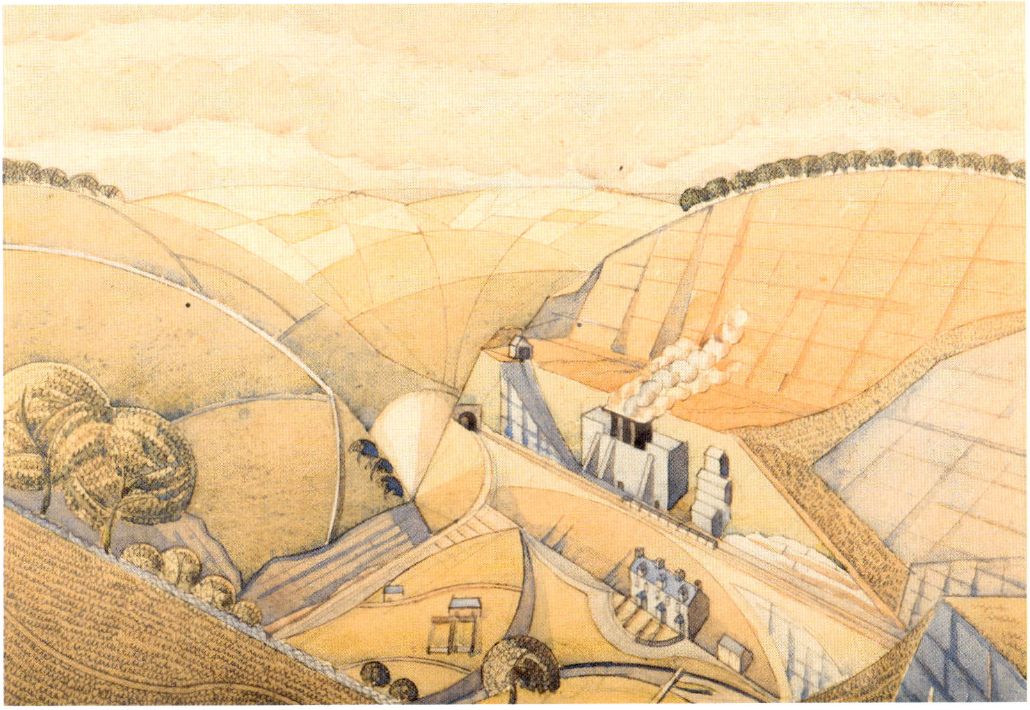

Karl Hagedorn (1889 - 1969)

Topley Pike, 1923

Signed and dated, pencil, pen and watercolour - 36 x 52 cm.

Trained in Manchester and on the Continent, Hagedorn moved to Buxton around the time of this painting. The carved geodetic forms of Topley Pike, a limestone quarry near Buxton, Derbyshire, lying inside the Peak District National Park, which would have appealed to Hagedorn's sense of Modernism. As Simon Martin has remarked, his watercolour landscapes from the 1920's 'encapsulate the search for solace in the landscape that appears in the work of so many others of his generation. These works have a distinctive clarity and call to mind Paul Nash's question of whether it was possible to 'Go Modern and Be British'. As an outsider, Hagedorn was not weighed down by such a sense of tradition. During the same period, he was also designing eye-catching posters... applying the lessons of European modernism to commercial advertising'.

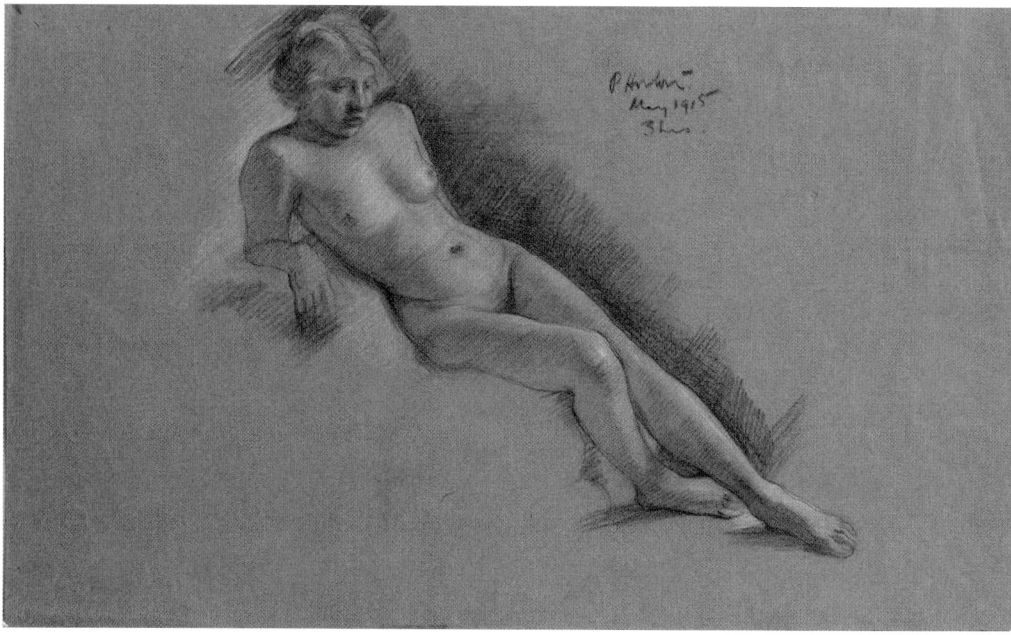

Percy Horton (1897-1970)

Reclining Nude, 1915

Signed and dated May 1915, inscribed 3 hours, coloured chalk and pastel on grey paper - 26 x 45 cm.

Born in Brighton, Percy Horton attended the School of Art there from 1912-1916. Drawings made in the Life Room, often as timed exercises (hence the 3 hours), formed a major part of all Art School curricula at this period. During WW1 he became a conscientious objector and was sentenced to two years hard labour in Carlton Prison, Edinburgh, from 1916-18.

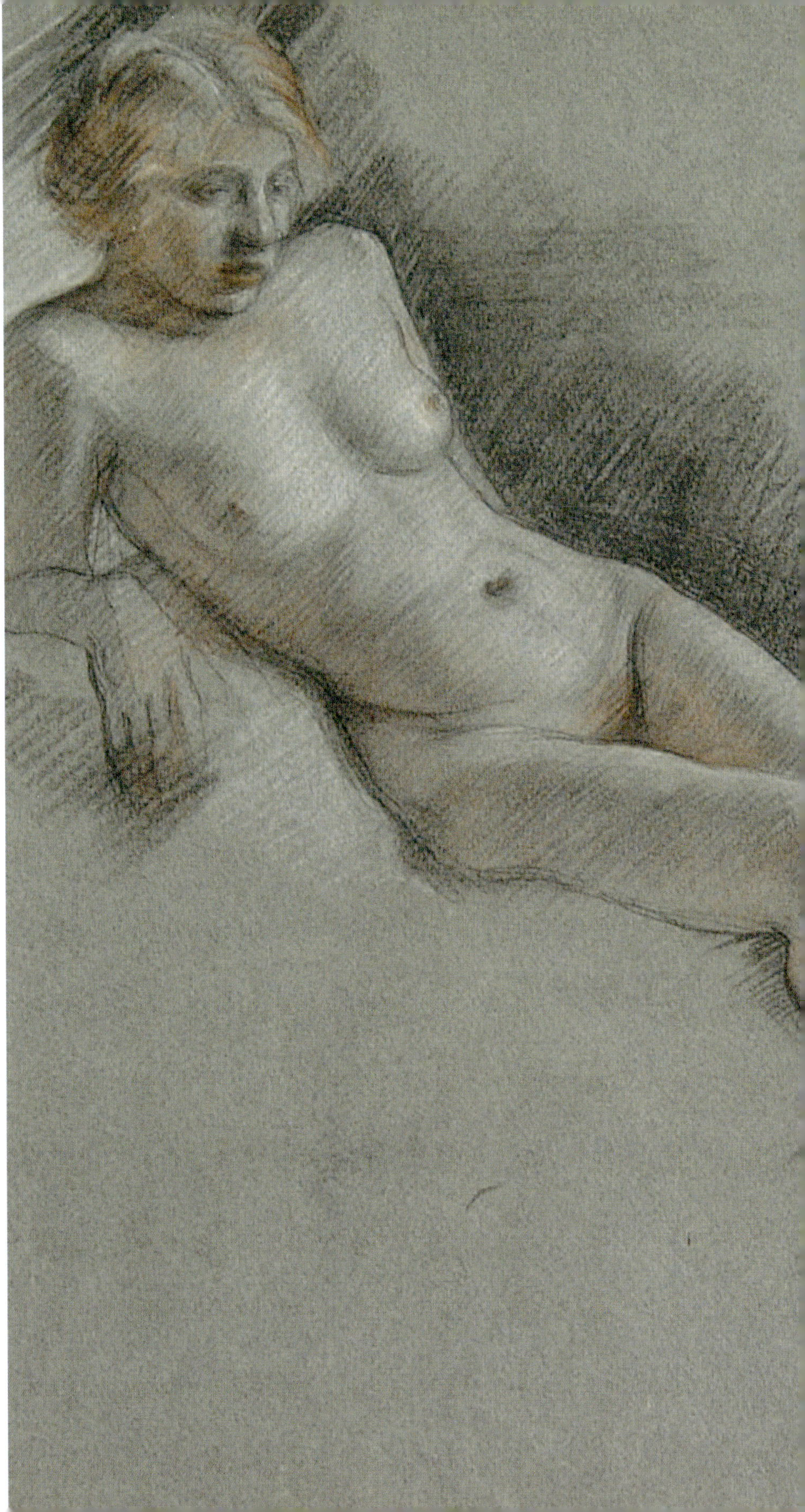

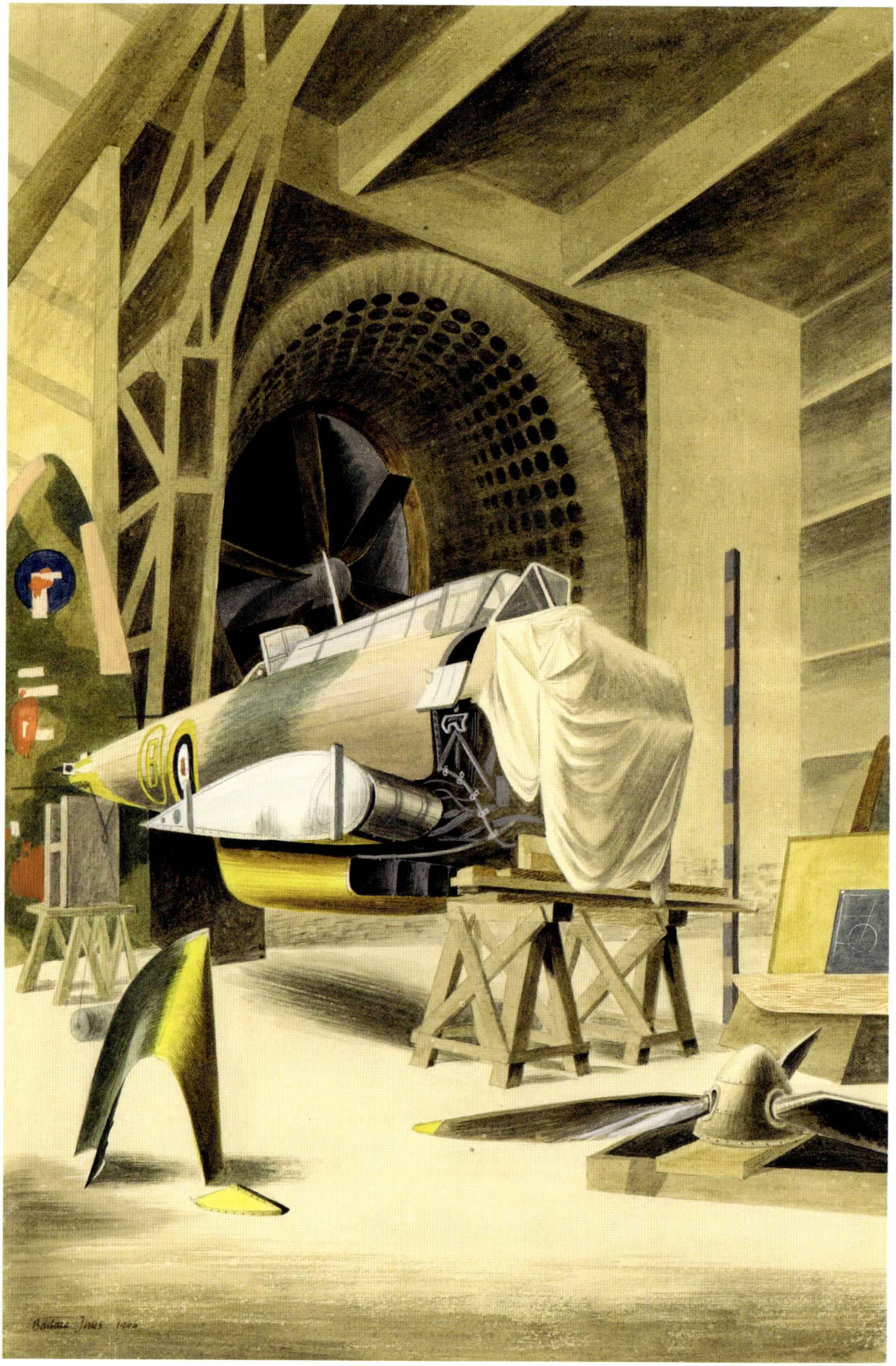

Barbara Jones (1912-1978)

The Wind Tunnel - Royal Aircraft Establishment Farnborough, 1944

Signed and dated, watercolour -56 x 35.5 cm.

This composition is closely related to one of Jones' Recording Britain watercolours in the collection of the Victoria & Albert Museum.

Recording Britain, which was intended to boost national morale during wartime by celebrating the country's heritage, was the brainchild of Kenneth Clark, who saw it as an extension of the Official War Artist scheme. By choosing watercolour painting as the medium of record, Clark hoped that the scheme would also help to preserve this characteristic English art form

The scheme employed several women, notably Barbara Jones and Enid Marx. There is no record of how Jones, still in her twenties, became involved in the *Recording Britain* Scheme but she was one of the first artists' to be commissioned and its most prolific contributor.

Lt Richard Barrett Talbot Kelly (1896-1971)

An RE8 with a French Nieuport 27 fighter escort, circa 1916

Watercolour - 103 x 68.5 cm.

This composition shows a British RE8, (a two-seat biplane reconnaissance aircraft), with a black band on the fuselage, escorted by a cream coloured Nieuport 27 (a French fighter aircraft). During WW1 Kelly fought at the battles of Festubert, Loos, 2nd Ypres and the Somme in 1916. He was blown up on August 5th during a bombardment and invalided home. After his recovery, he returned to France in March 1918 to study concealment techniques and then came back to England to become 'Specialist Instructor in Camouflage' at the School of Artillery at Larkhill. His interest in flying was such that he applied to be trained as a pilot. He was posted to the Royal Flying School at Reading but the war ended just as he was about to join his training squadron.

A book entitled *'A Subaltern's Odyssey, A Memoir of the Great War 1915-1917'* was published in 1980 based on Richard Talbot Kelly's diaries.

Similar compositions by Kelly are in the collection of the RAF Museum, Hendon, though this - the largest recorded work of its kind - is unique in its format.

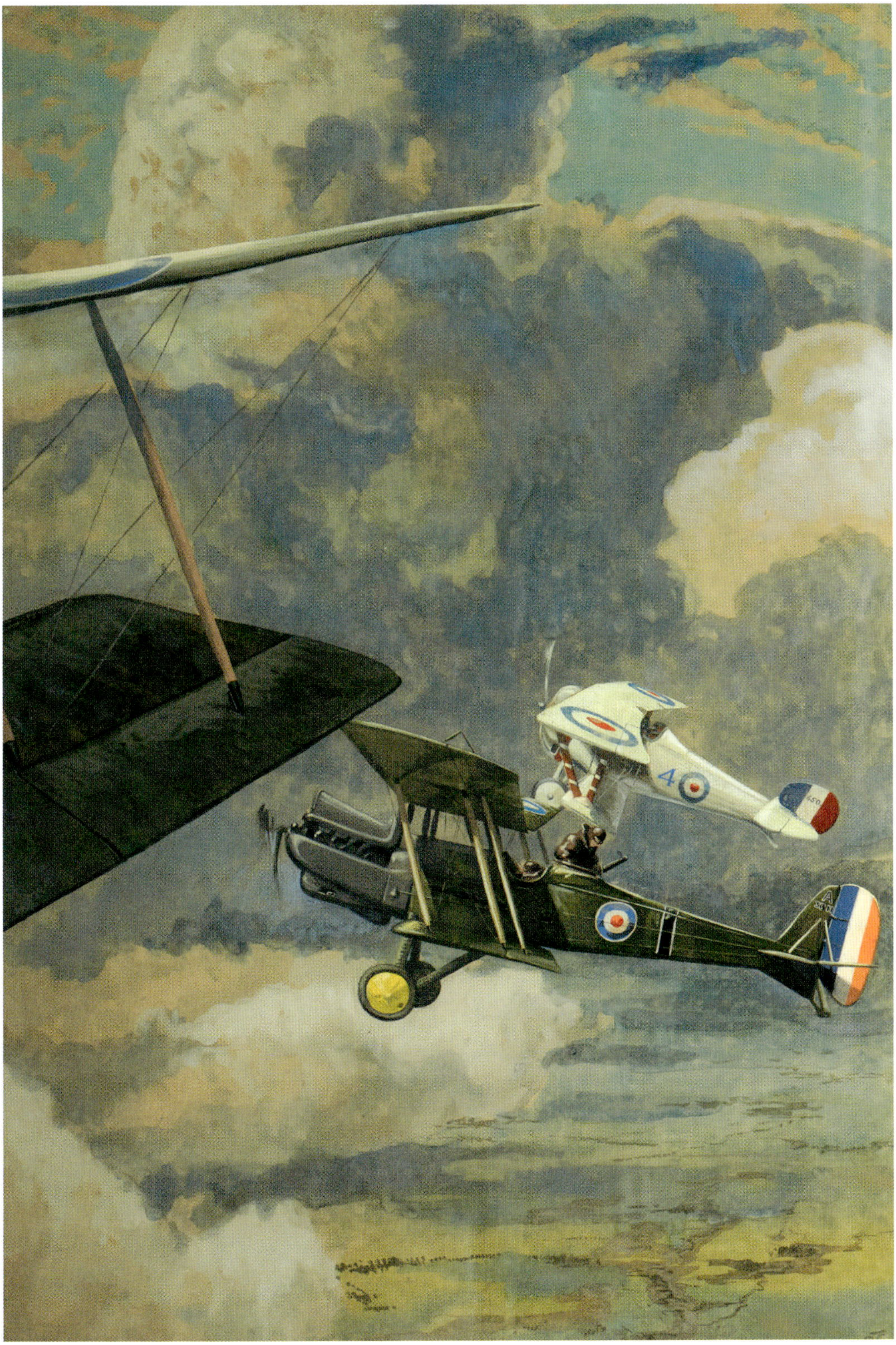
4

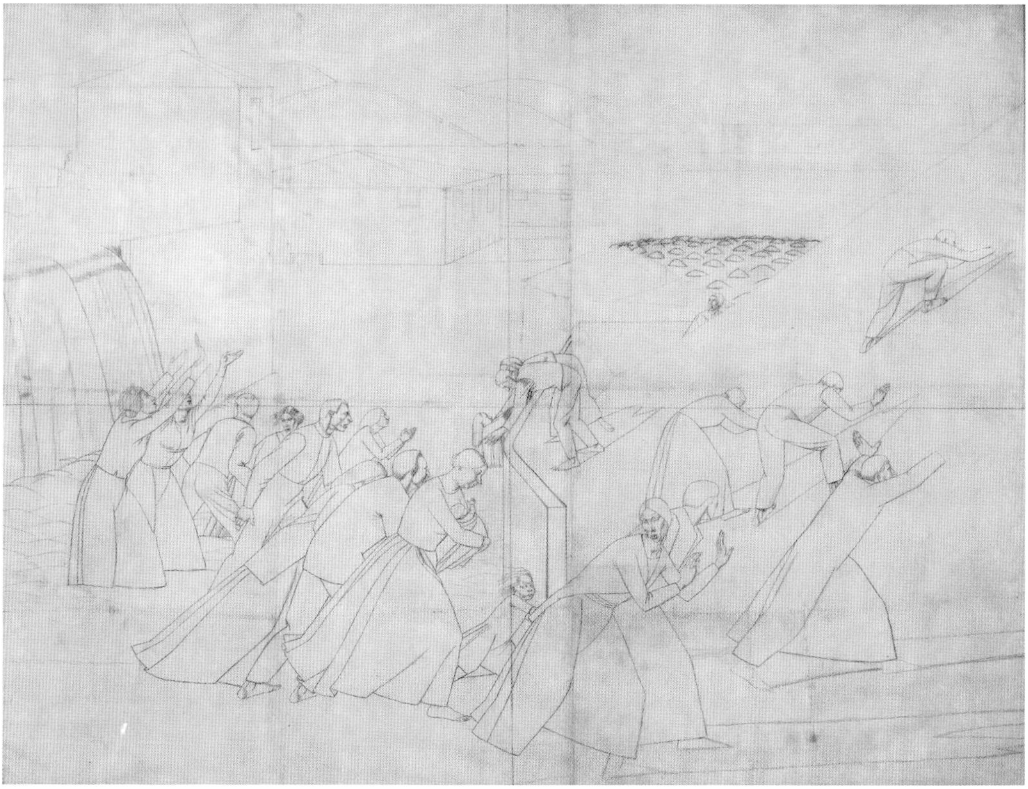

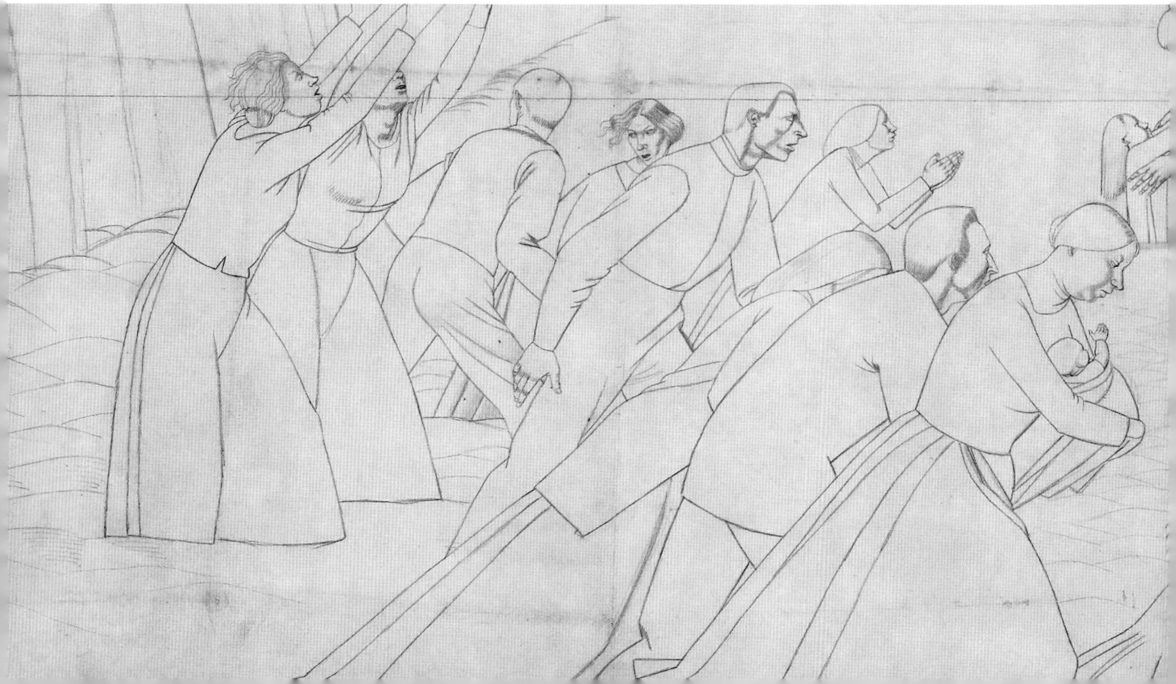

Winifred Knights (1899-1947)

The original cartoon for The Deluge, 1920

Pencil on tracing paper - 152.4 x 183 cm.

The Deluge was Winifred Knights' winning entry for the Prix de Rome in 1920. The Scholarship rules required that the painting was produced in oil or tempera, together with a cartoon, both of which were to be executed in eight weeks. On this full-size cartoon, the lines are heavily scored into the tracing paper so that the outline could be transferred onto the same size canvas, now one of the prize possessions of Tate Britain. The artist's mother modelled for the central figure carrying the baby and the artist Arnold Mason, to whom Knights was at the time engaged, modelled for the man shinning up the hill. The artist portrayed herself as the figure to the centre right of the composition.

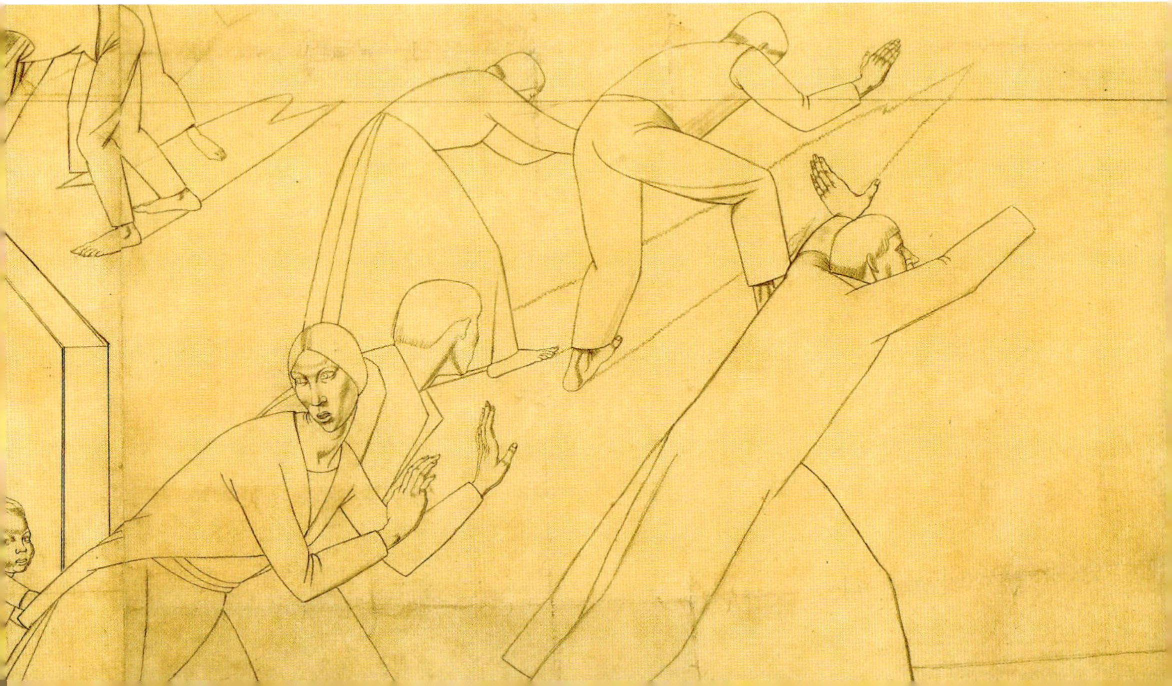

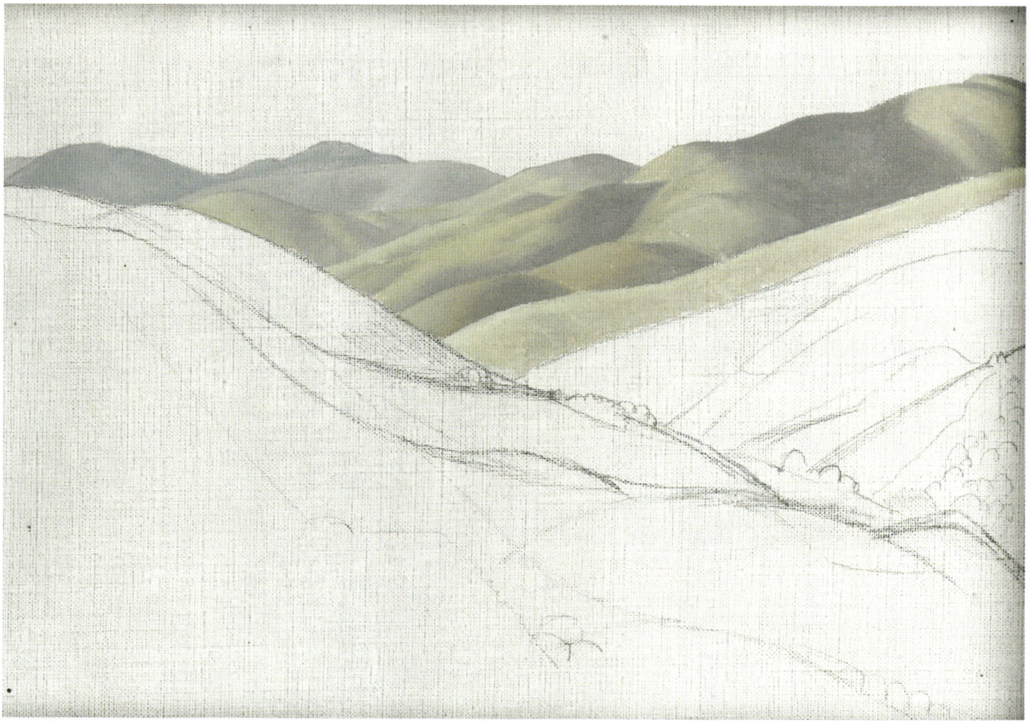

Winifred Knights (1899-1947)

Italian Landscape, circa 1924

Oil and pencil on canvas - 15.6 x 21 cm.

Winifred Knights' painstaking paintings in oil were always preceded by meticulous drawings and studies in oil and then transferred to canvas.

Writing from Italy to her Aunt Millicent Murby Knights confided that she was 'in love with the mountains'.

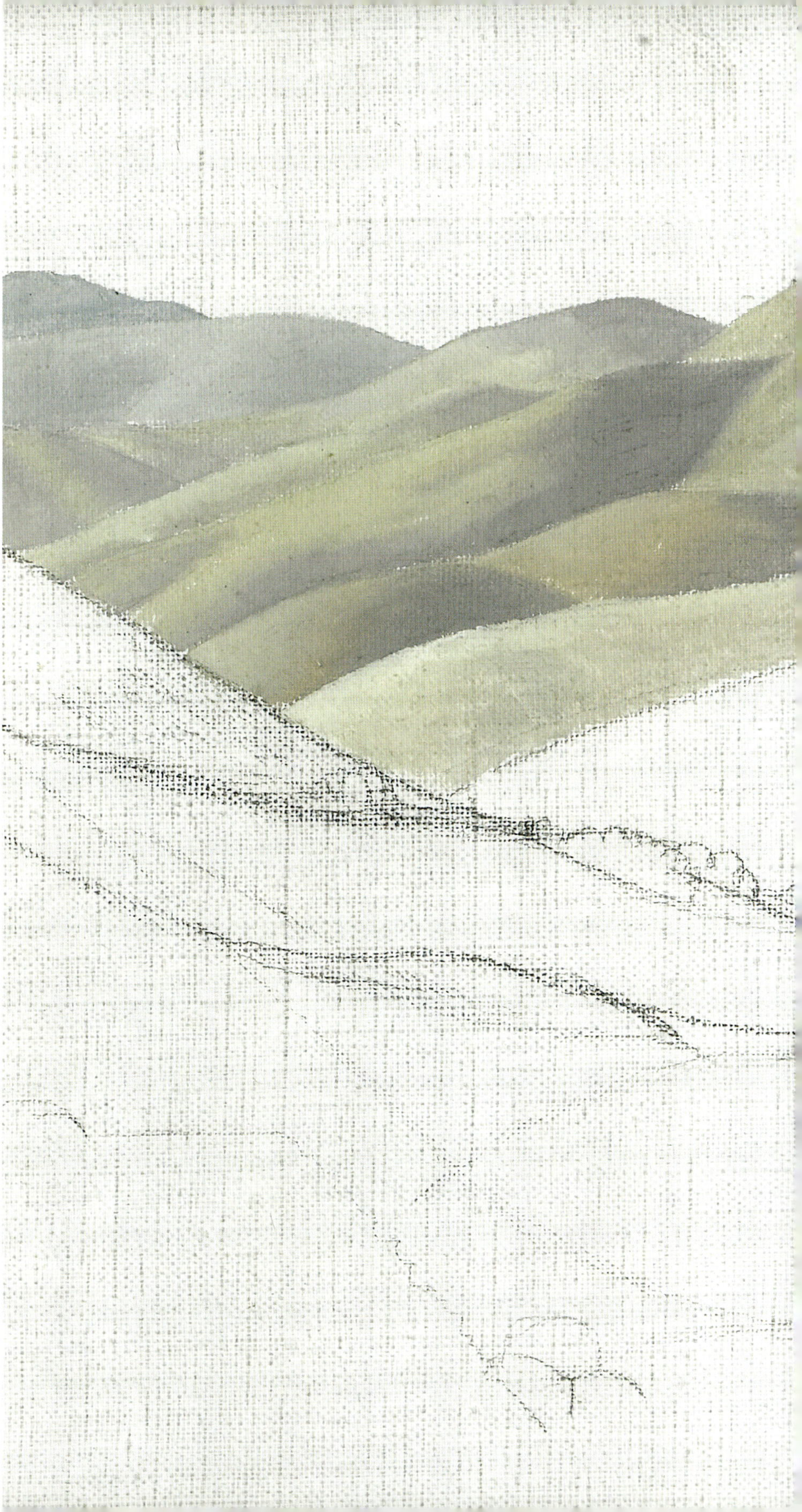

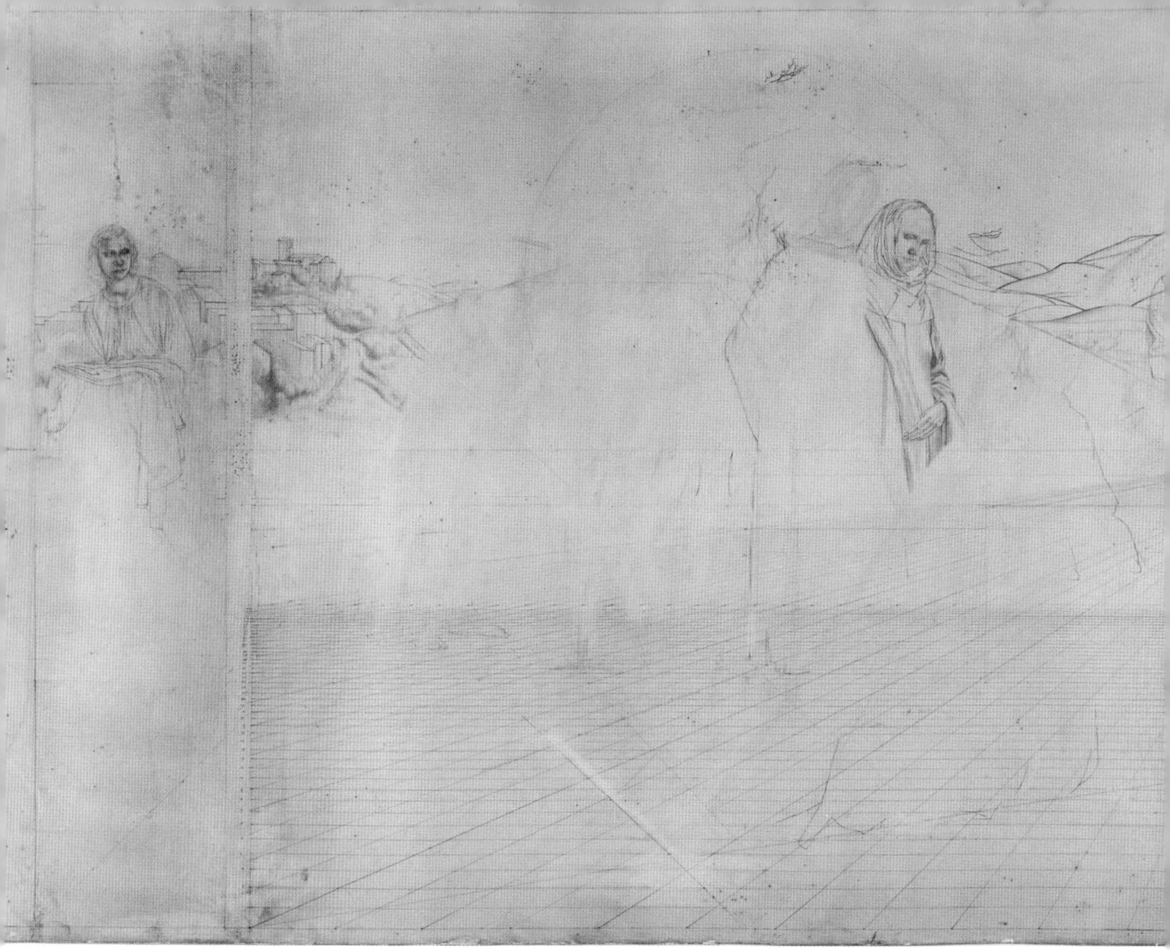

Winifred Knights (1899-1947)

Cartoon for Scenes from the Life of Saint Martin of Tours, 1932

Pencil - 76 x 188 cm.

Knights was commissioned to paint the Milner Memorial altarpiece for Canterbury Cathedral, by Bishop Bell in 1928 ; she painted it some five years later in 1933. It was to be the last major work completed by Knights. This full-sized cartoon with its pin holes and lattice work of perspective lines bare witness to her meticulous working methods through which each section of the composition was transferred to the canvas using tracing paper. The obvious pleasure Knights took in certain passages is evident in the attention lavished on sections of the landscape, the angel's wings and the drapery.

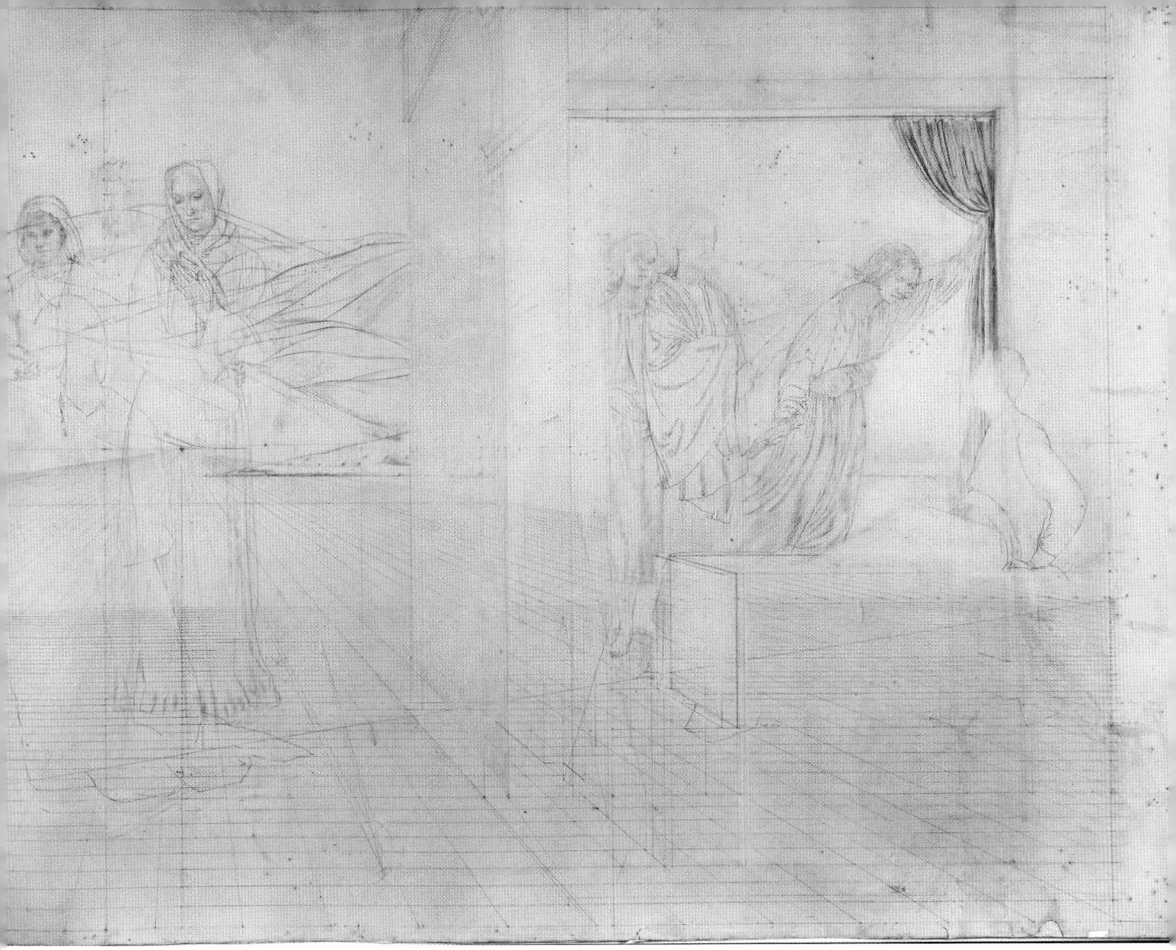

Bishop Bell, who was involved with commissions for religious works from numerous artists (including Vanessa Bell, Duncan Grant, Augustus Lunn and Hans Feibusch), described the St Martin Altarpiece, in The Studio, September 1942, as '*one of the most lovely, delicate and deeply felt modern religious paintings that I know.*'.

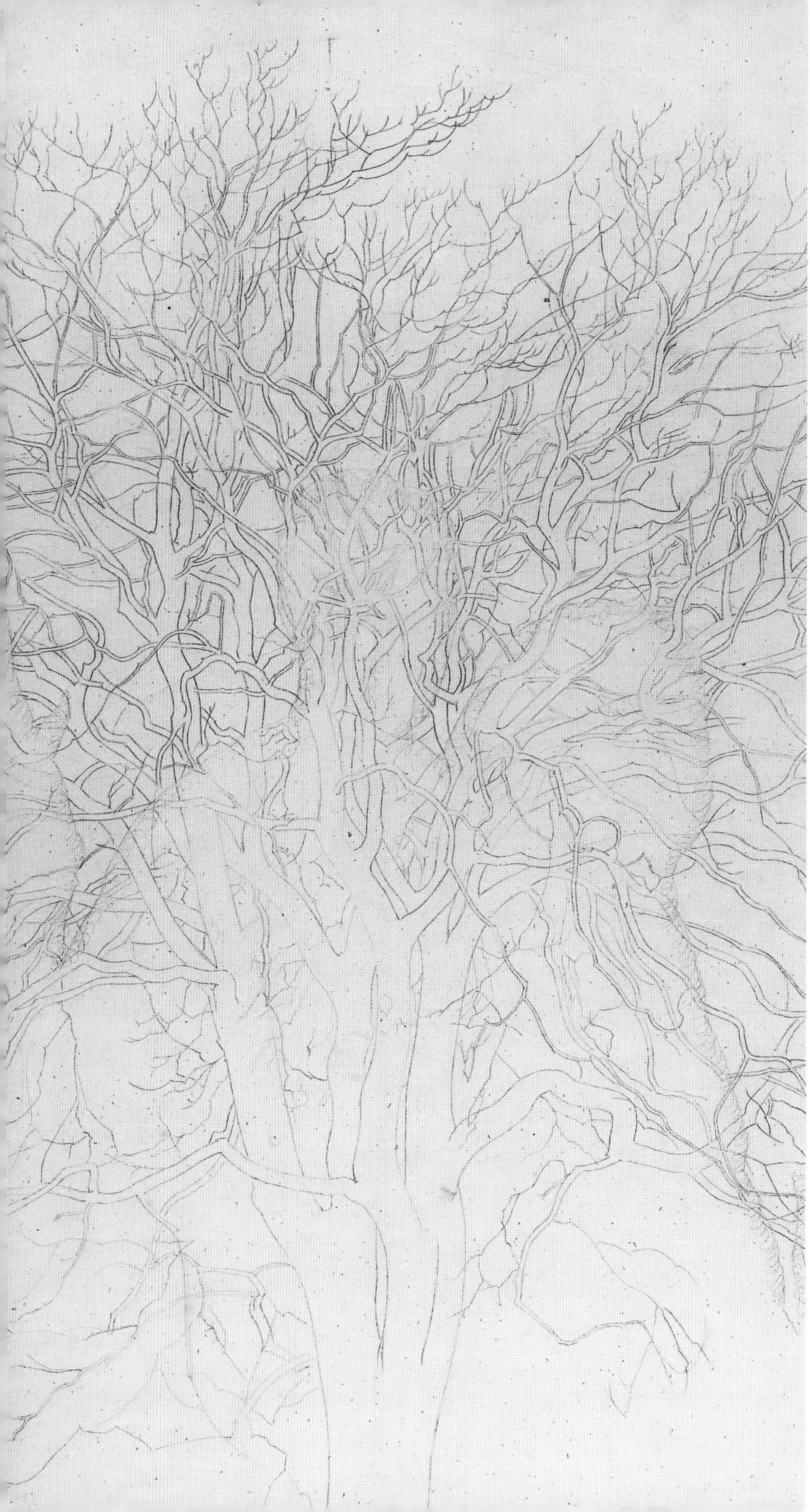

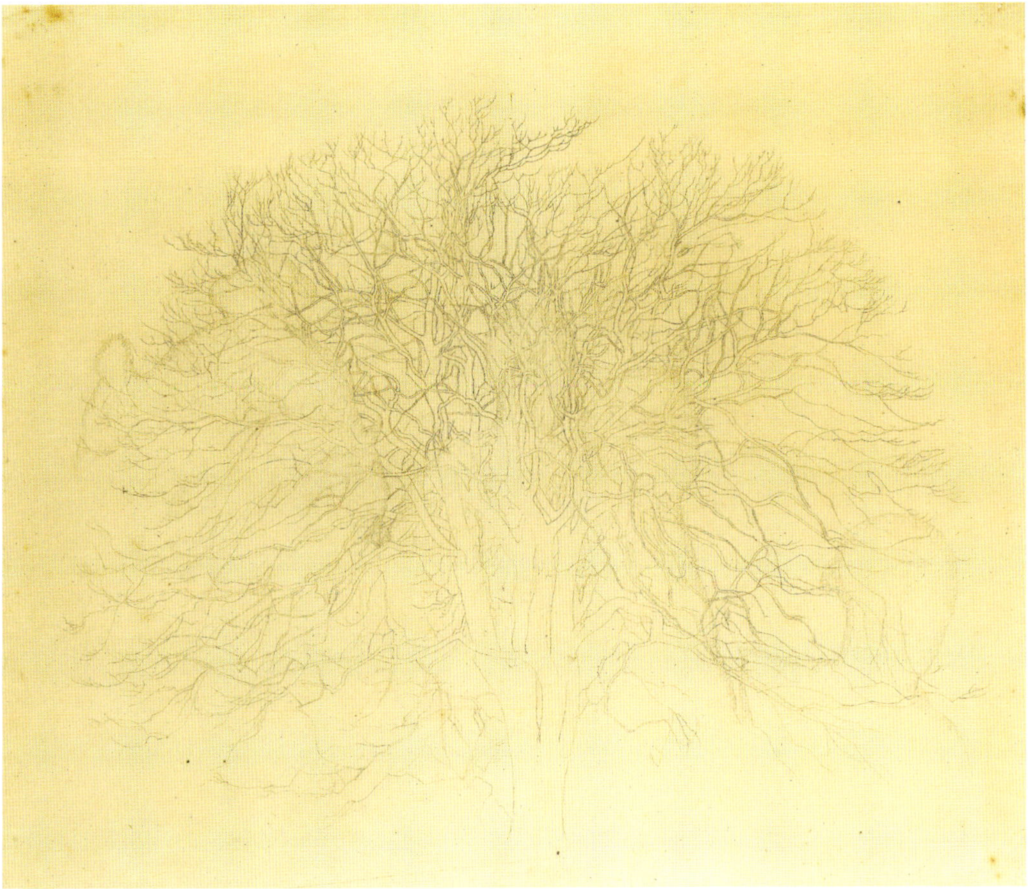

Winifred Knights (1899-1947)

Study of a Walnut tree for Scenes from the Life of Saint Martin of Tours, circa 1930

Pencil on tracing paper - 43.3 x 49.4 cm.

In Christian theology the walnut symbolises the redemptive work of Christ. According to Knights the tree's bare branches 'locate the scene during the more than usually severe winter' in which Saint Martin shared his cloak with a beggar, thus allowing the viewer a comparison between the cycle of nature and the Christian narrative. 'I am doing some sketches of trees before they burst their buds. It is a race against time for all the trees are rapidly changing but happily I have chosen a Walnut tree which is slower than the rest'.

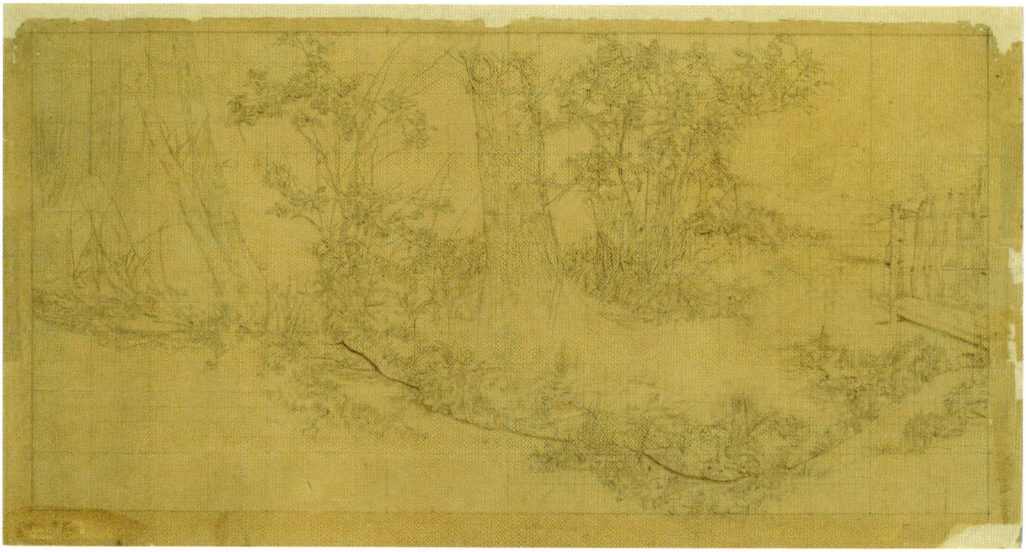

Winifred Knights (1899-1947)

Compositional study for The Flight into Egypt, circa 1938

Pencil, pen and ink on tracing paper - 48.3 x 89 cm.

In 1937, Knights was commissioned by the Earl of Crawford and Balcarres to produce a large Decorative Painting (6 x 10 ft) of the Flight into Egypt for Balcarres Castle. The narrative was set on the banks of a stream covered in bluebells. By the time WW2 was declared, Knights had partially completed the painting, with studies of the riverbank and foliage rendered with elaborate and minute detail. As a result of Knights' sudden death in 1947, the painting was never realised.

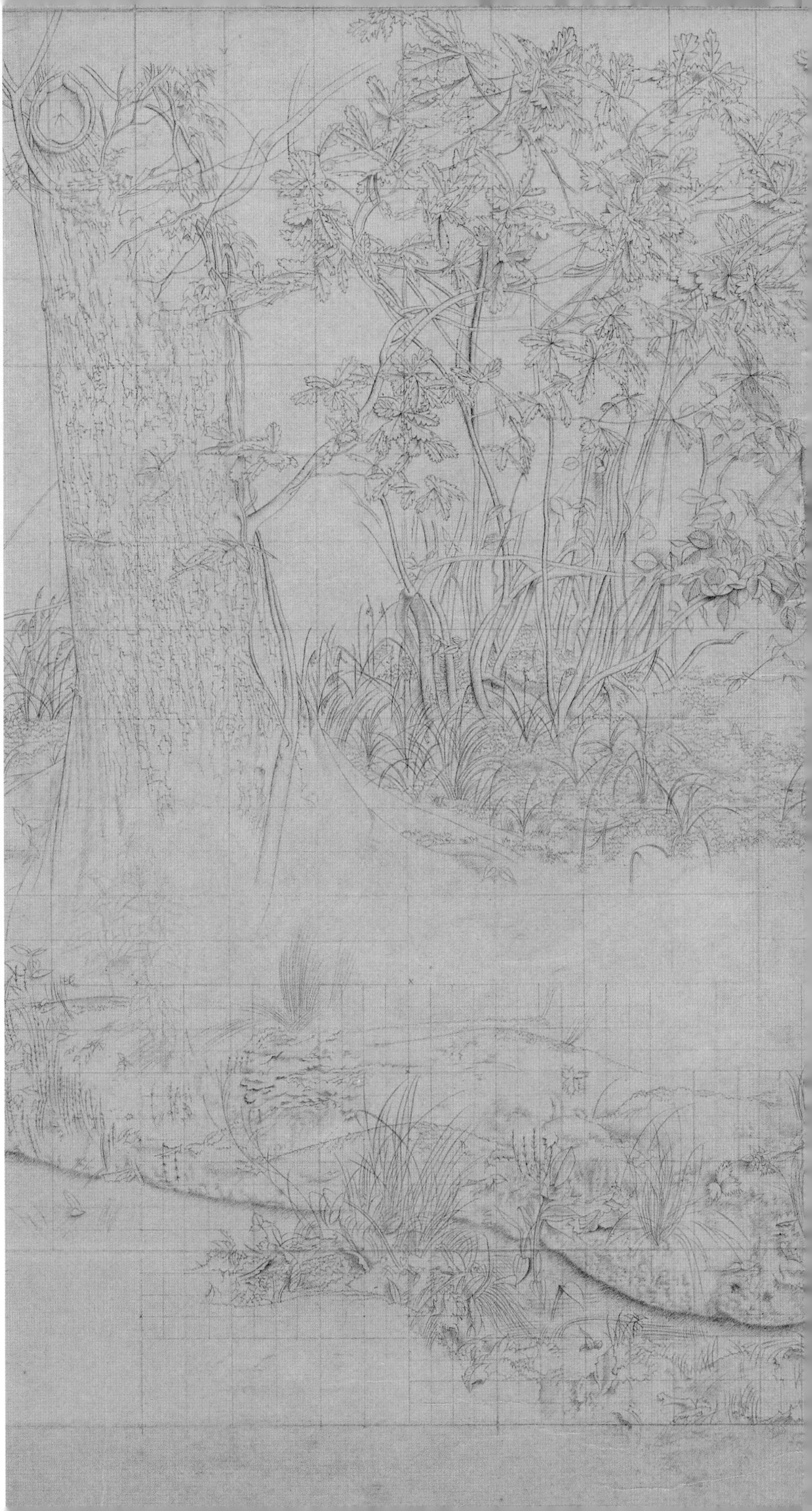

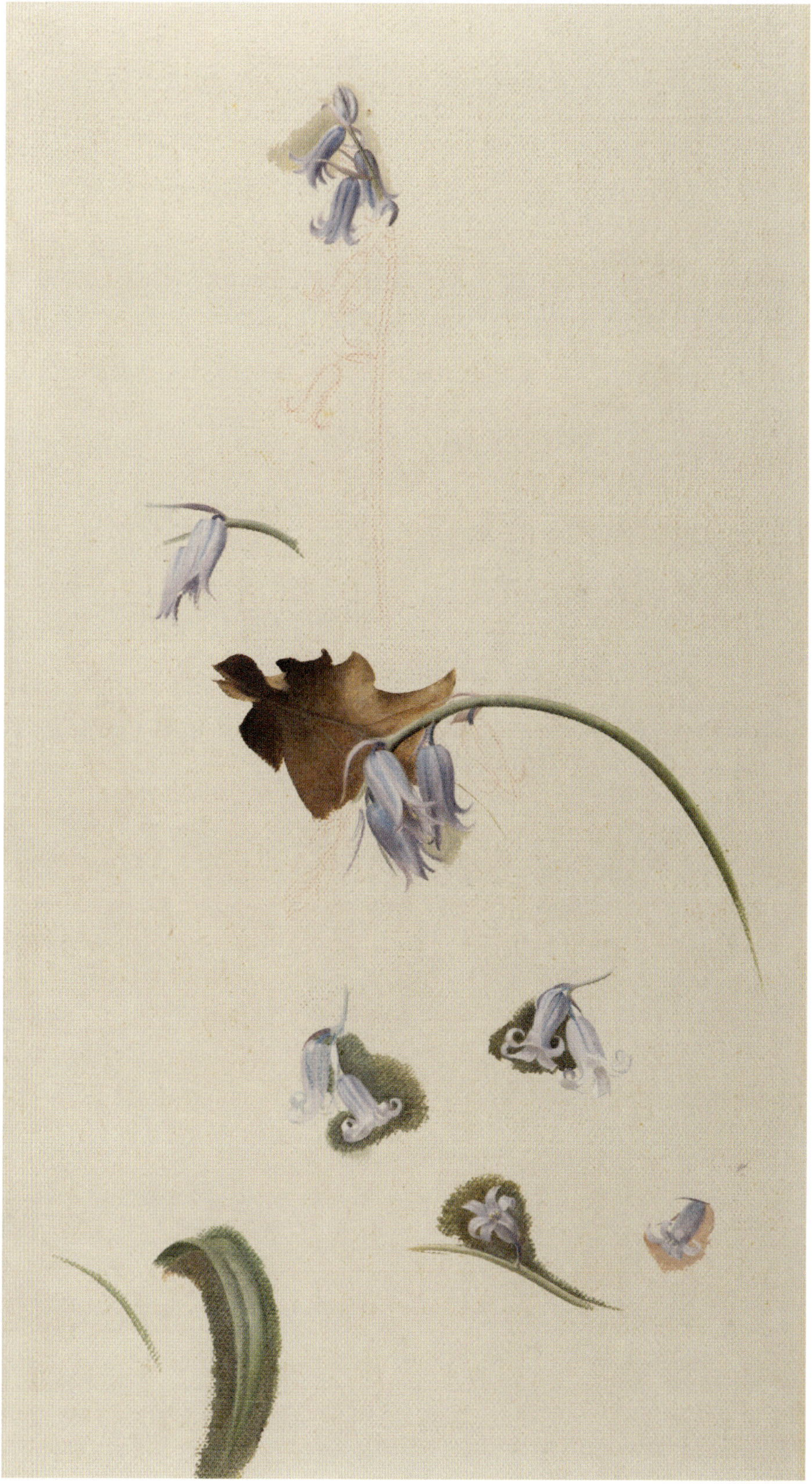

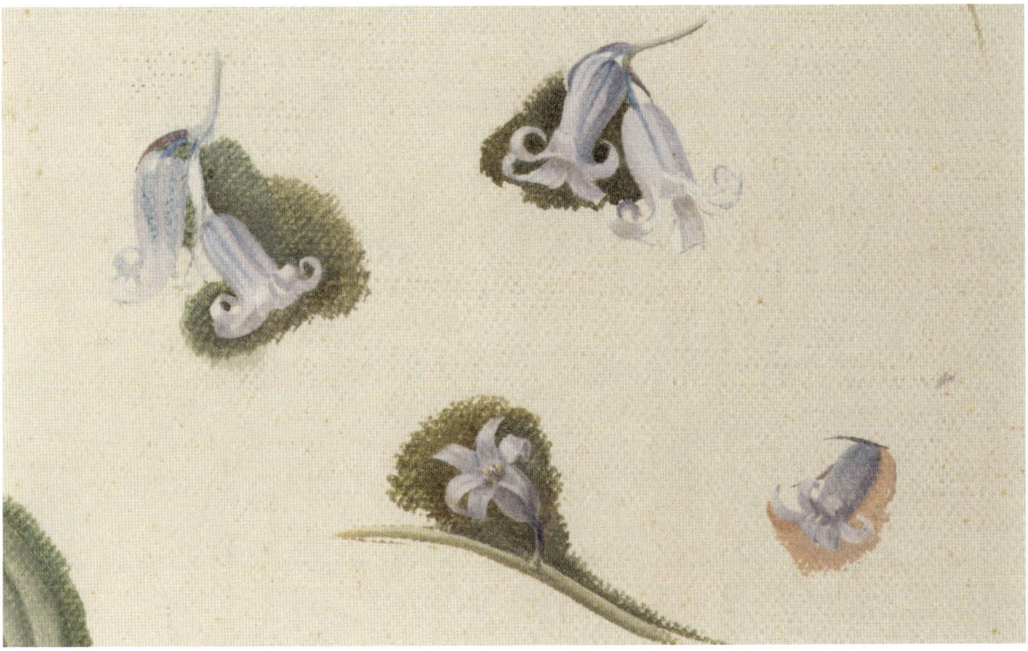

Winifred Knights (1899-1947)

Study of Bluebells, circa 1937

Tempera on canvas over red pencil - 43 x 25 cm.

When the artist Sir D. Y. Cameron saw Knights' studies for The Flight, he admired her intensity of observation: 'The artist of today might laugh at my love and admiration of her work, so far removed from the spirit of our times', he wrote. 'But it is timeless and of another world'.

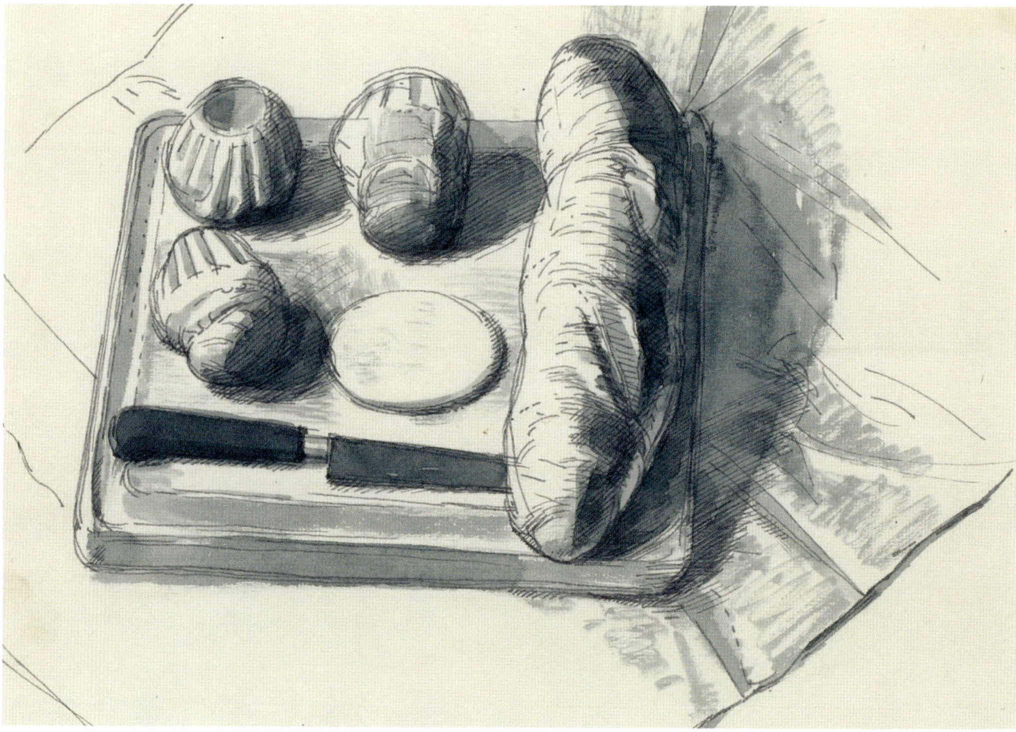

Charles Mahoney (1903-1968)

Still life of bread, brioche and a knife, circa 1935

Pen and blue ink, blue wash - 25.5 x 35.5 cm.

Mahoney's love of drawing owed much to four years spent at The Royal College of Art, starting with a Scholarship in 1922. Under the guidance of its Principal, Sir William Rothenstein, Mahoney came to believe that drawing was a vital basic skill which, according to his daughter, Elizabeth Bulkeley, '*underpinned other disciplines and which would be of use whether an artist worked figuratively or otherwise*'. Much of Mahoney's own career was spent in passing on his knowledge as a teacher at The Royal College of Art from 1928-1953.

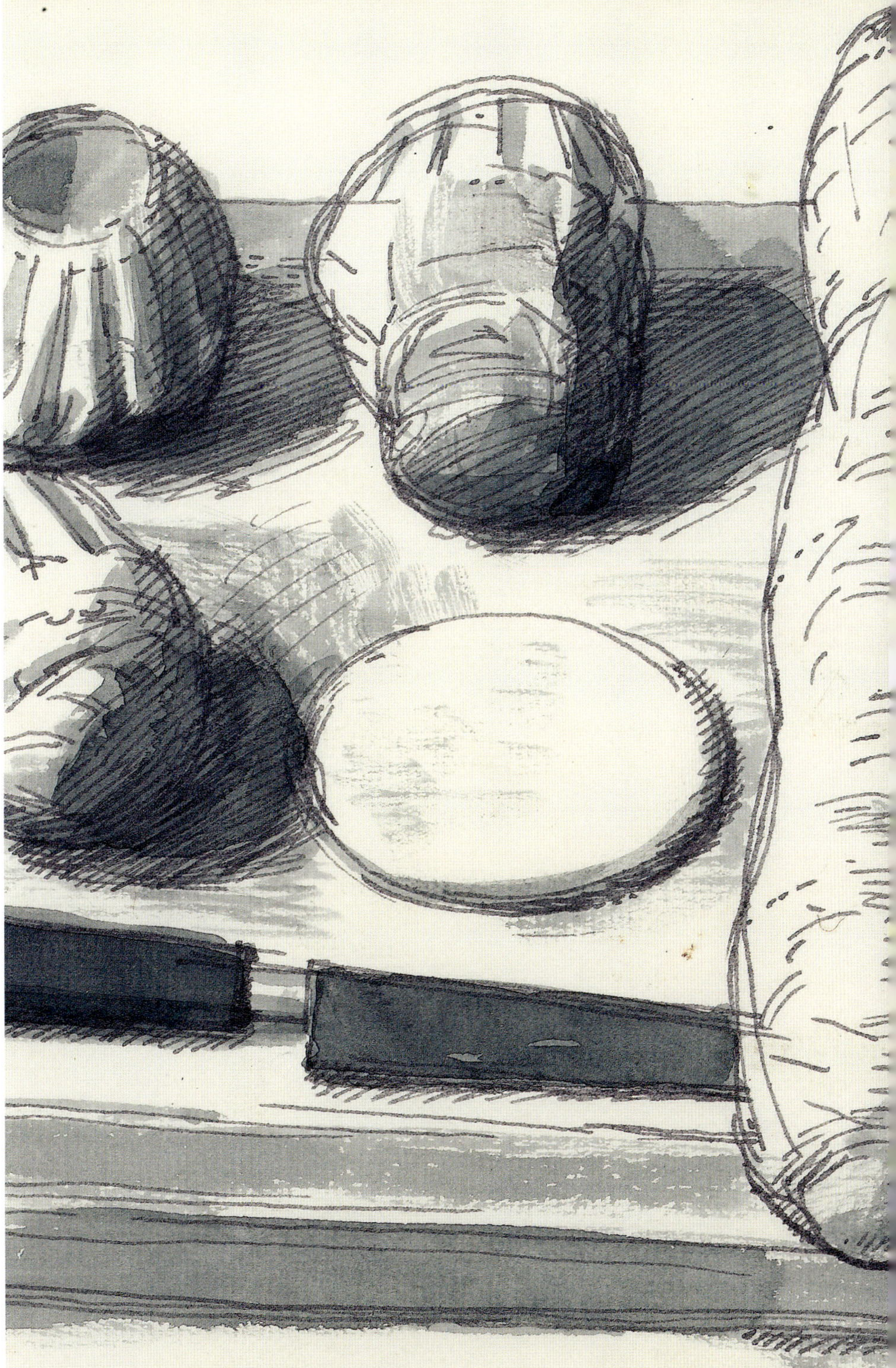

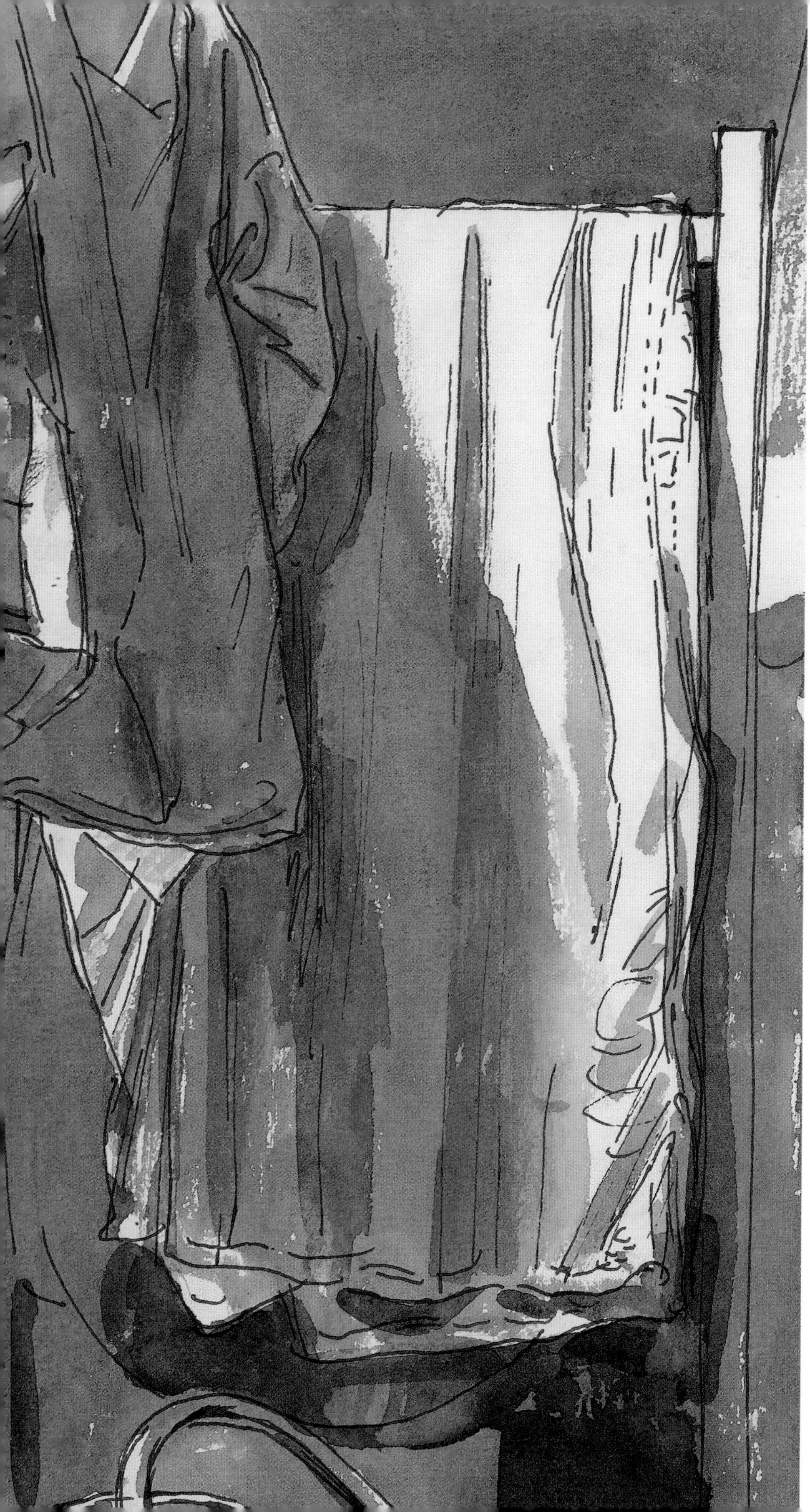

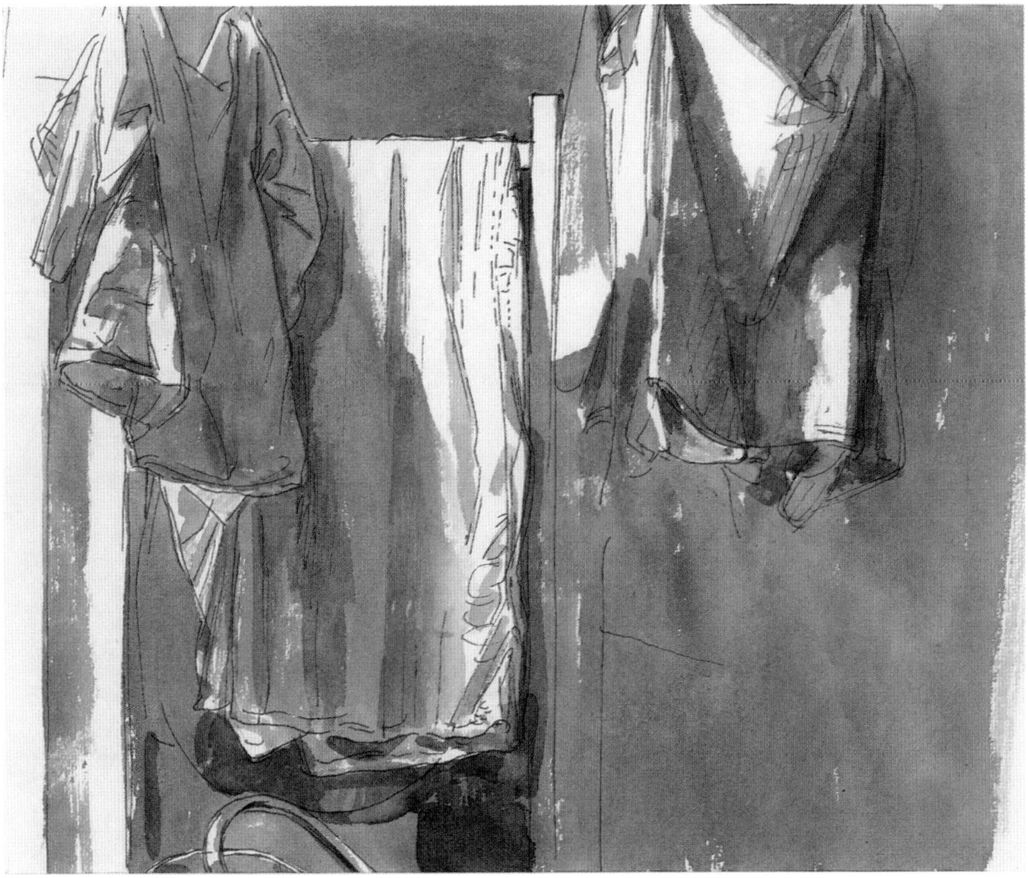

Charles Mahoney (1903-1968)

Washing Hanging to Dry, circa 1941

Pen and ink and wash - 29.5 x 35 cm.

Mahoney's admiration for Tiepolo is especially evident in his ink and wash drawings. He favoured a textured paper, soft to the touch, such as Ingres, or hand-made papers from firms such as Hayle Mill or Barcham Green. For his drawings he preferred carbon pencils and used charcoal, adding white or red crayons as highlights, and he also developed a great facility using pen and wash, taking trouble to mix and dilute his inks until he achieved the required tone and colour. His drawing pens were either reservoir nibs in holders or else cartridge pens.

Charles Mahoney (1903-1968)

Greenhouse Interior, circa 1935

Gouache - 57.3 x 39.4 cm.

Mahoney's unbridled enthusiasm for plants extended to include the objects and implements found in gardens such as watering cans, greenhouses, wheelbarrows and spades. His interest and aesthetic sensibilities were shared with his contemporaries Edward Bawden, Eric Ravilious, Geoffrey Rhoades, John Nash and Evelyn Dunbar, with whom he swapped cuttings by post. Mahoney was instrumental in helping Bawden lay out his celebrated garden at Brick House. Writing in the introduction to his book, *Gardener's Choice*, 1936 (co-authored and co-illustrated with Evelyn Dunbar) Mahoney stated: 'In addition to our natural pleasure in beautiful plants and our experience in raising and cultivating them, we have gained a close intimacy through drawing and painting them. We have observed them as artists as well as gardeners, and have necessarily been made aware not only of the garden value of a plant and the intrinsic beauty of its flower, but of proportions, forms and contrasts, of the subtle relations of the leaf to the bloom, or the plant to its neighbour.'

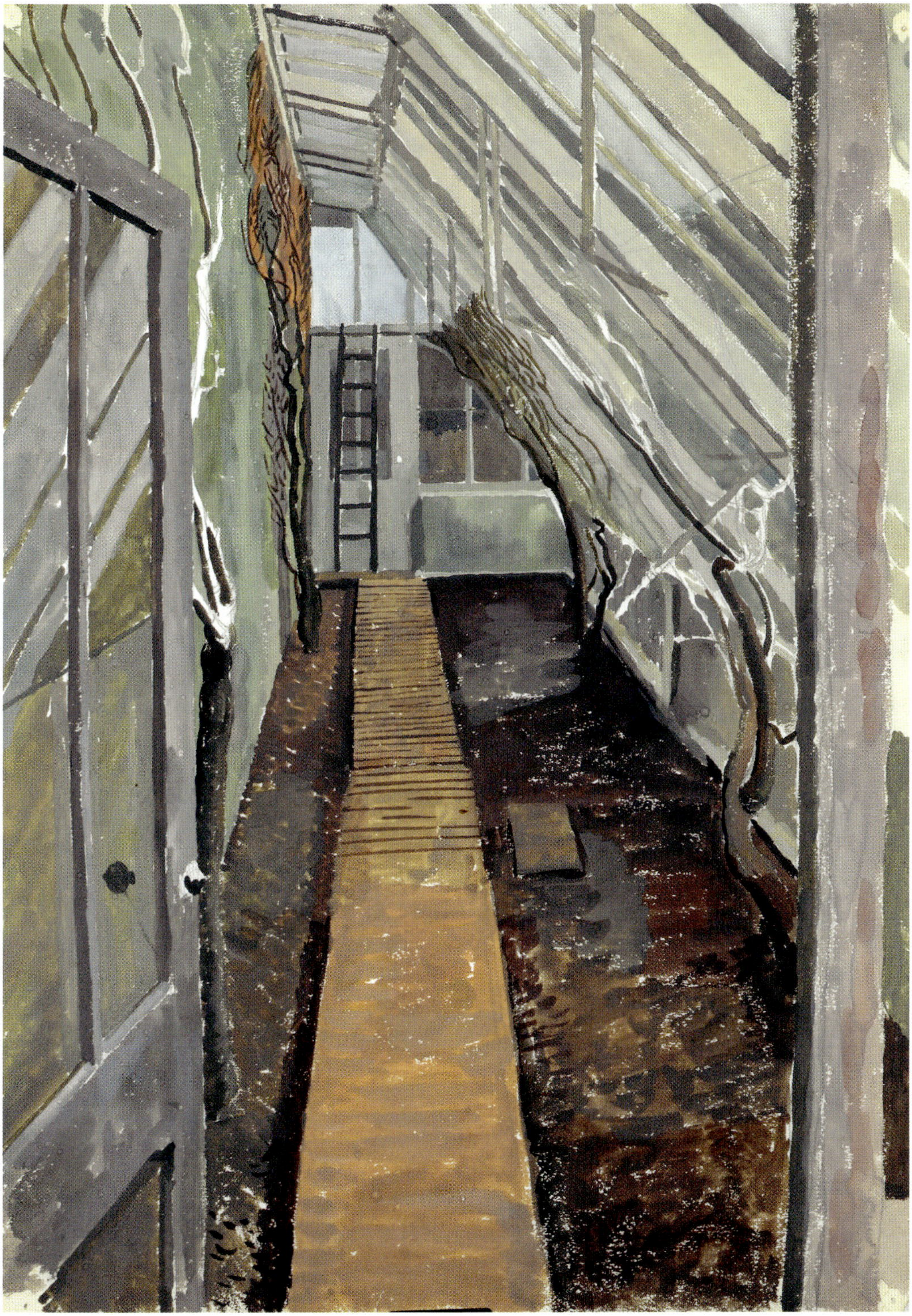

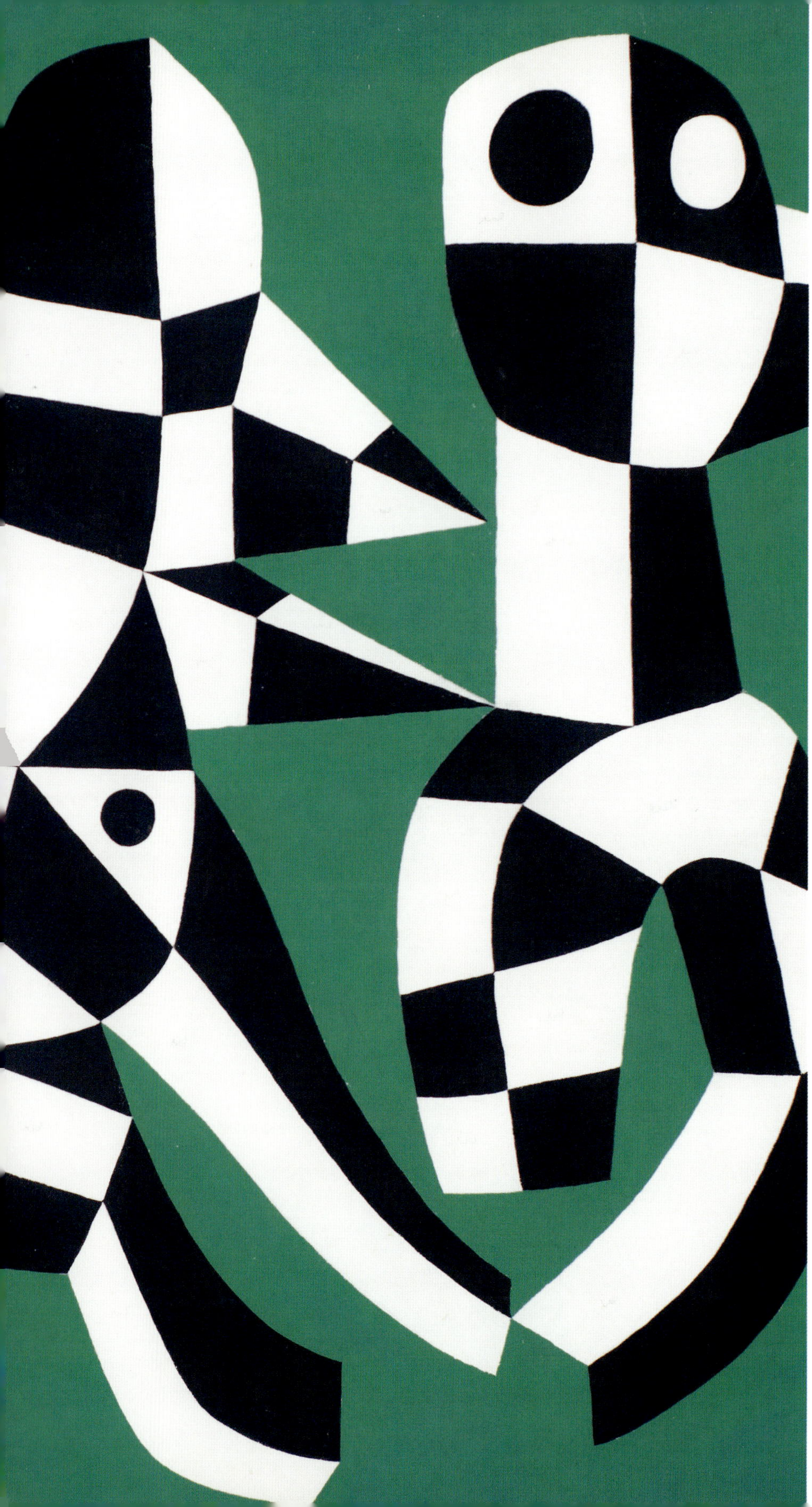

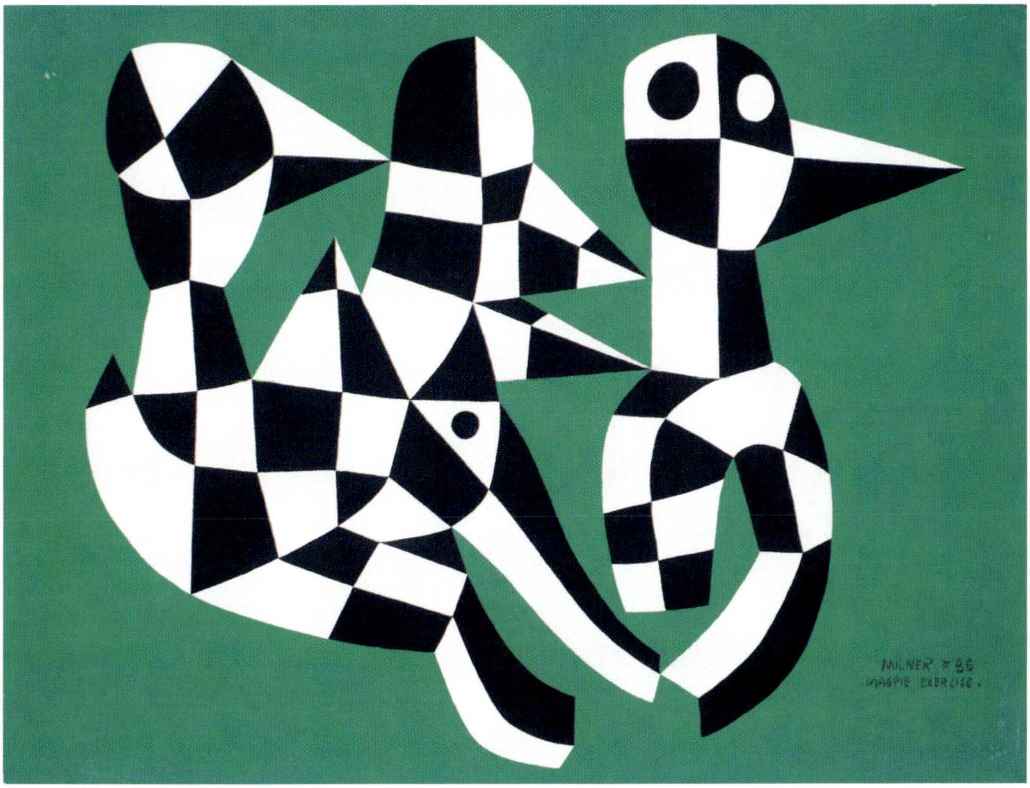

Alan Milner (1910-1984)

Magpie Exercise (F85), circa 1960

Gouache - 38.1 x 55.8 cm.

Milner composed his works using interacting figures reduced to abstract patterns. Each composition was based on a careful outline drawing with contrasting colour fields then added, usually in gouache. In spite of the intriguing title of this work Milner mostly preferred simply using a number, prefixed by a letter, alongside his signature, to title his works.

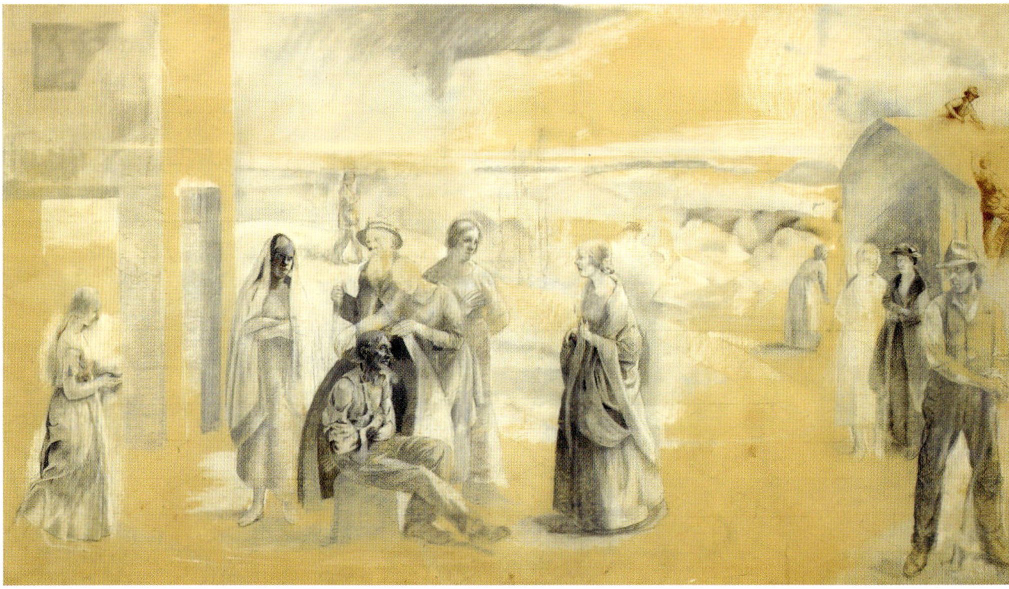

Sir Thomas Monnington (1902-1976)

Cartoon for Winter, circa 1921

Chalk and gouache on brown paper - 122 x 216 cm.

Winter was Monnington's winning submission for the 1922 British School at Rome Scholarship in Decorative Painting. The four finalists were given eight weeks to produce a full-sized cartoon, colour studies and a finished canvas of a specified size, on the theme of Winter. Although considerably younger than the other entrants the judges, including John Singer Sargent and George Clausen, were especially impressed by Monnington's cartoon. The landscape is based on studies looking towards Clearbury Ring near Salisbury. The models include, (on the left-hand side) a self-portrait holding an axe, with the artist's mother behind.

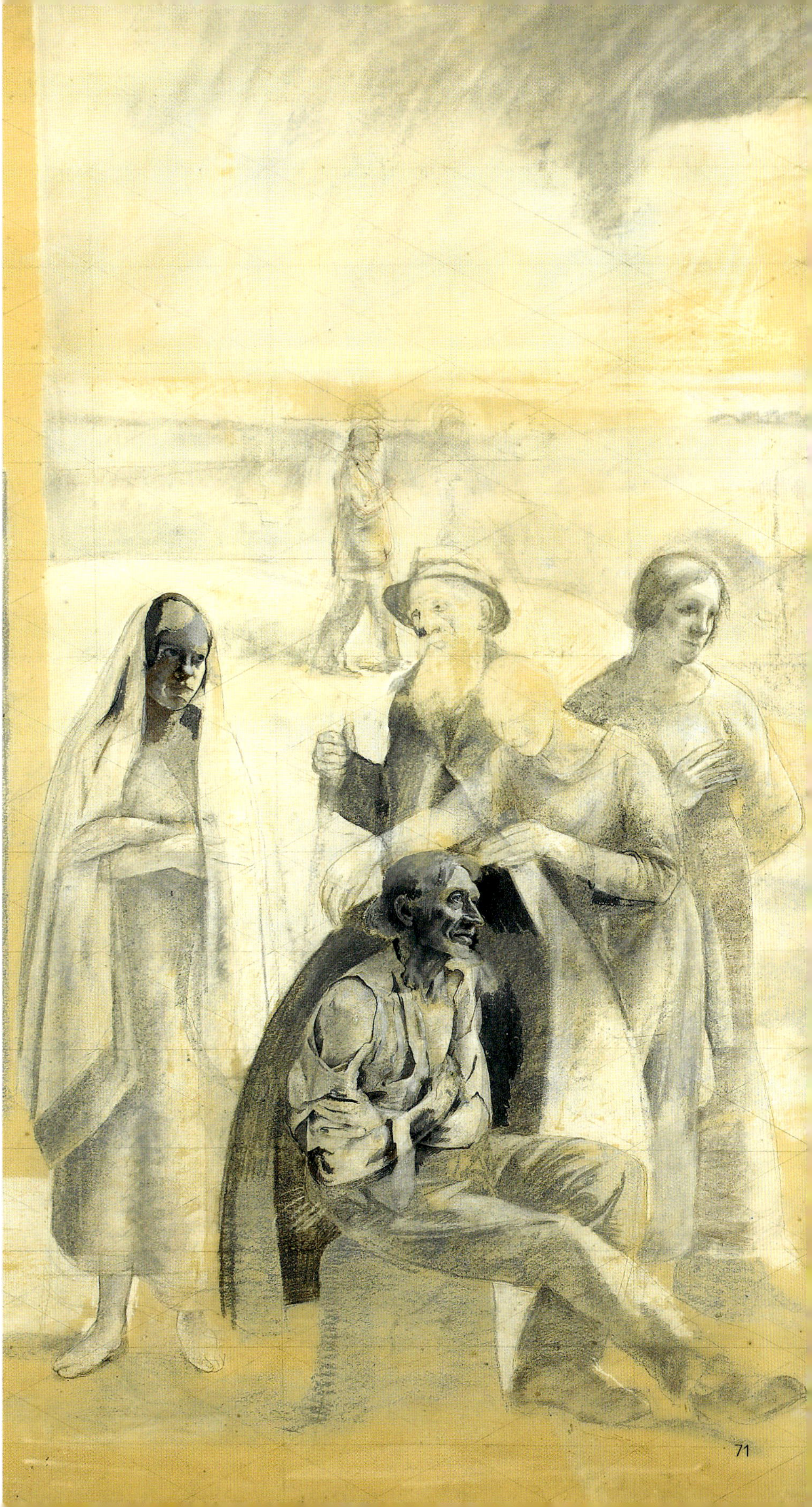

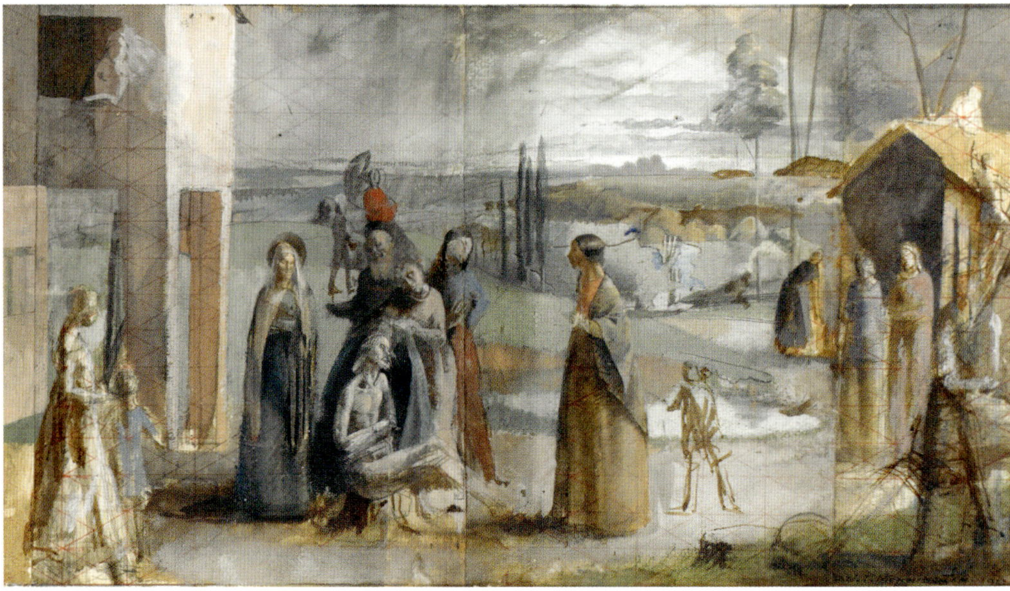

Sir Thomas Monnington (1902-1976)

Study for Winter, 1922

Gouache, squared - 21 x 37 cm.

Colour studies were an essential part of the Rome Scholarship competition. Monnington elected to use a closely controlled palette. Writing in The Observer in 1922 P.C. Konody praised Monnington's painting for being 'steeped in the best traditions of the Italian Renaissance. His colour is dull, but there is a marked sense of style in his design'.

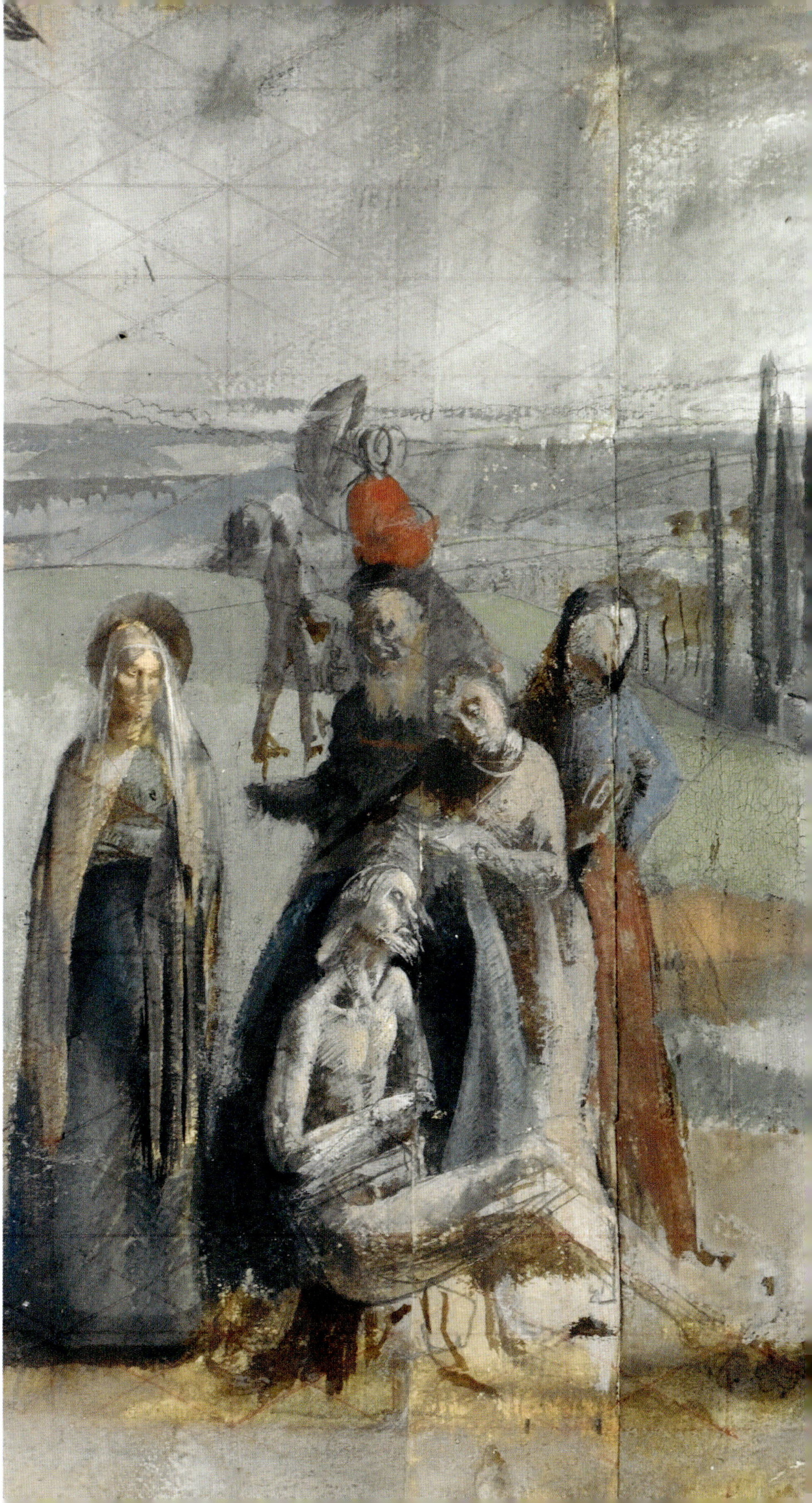

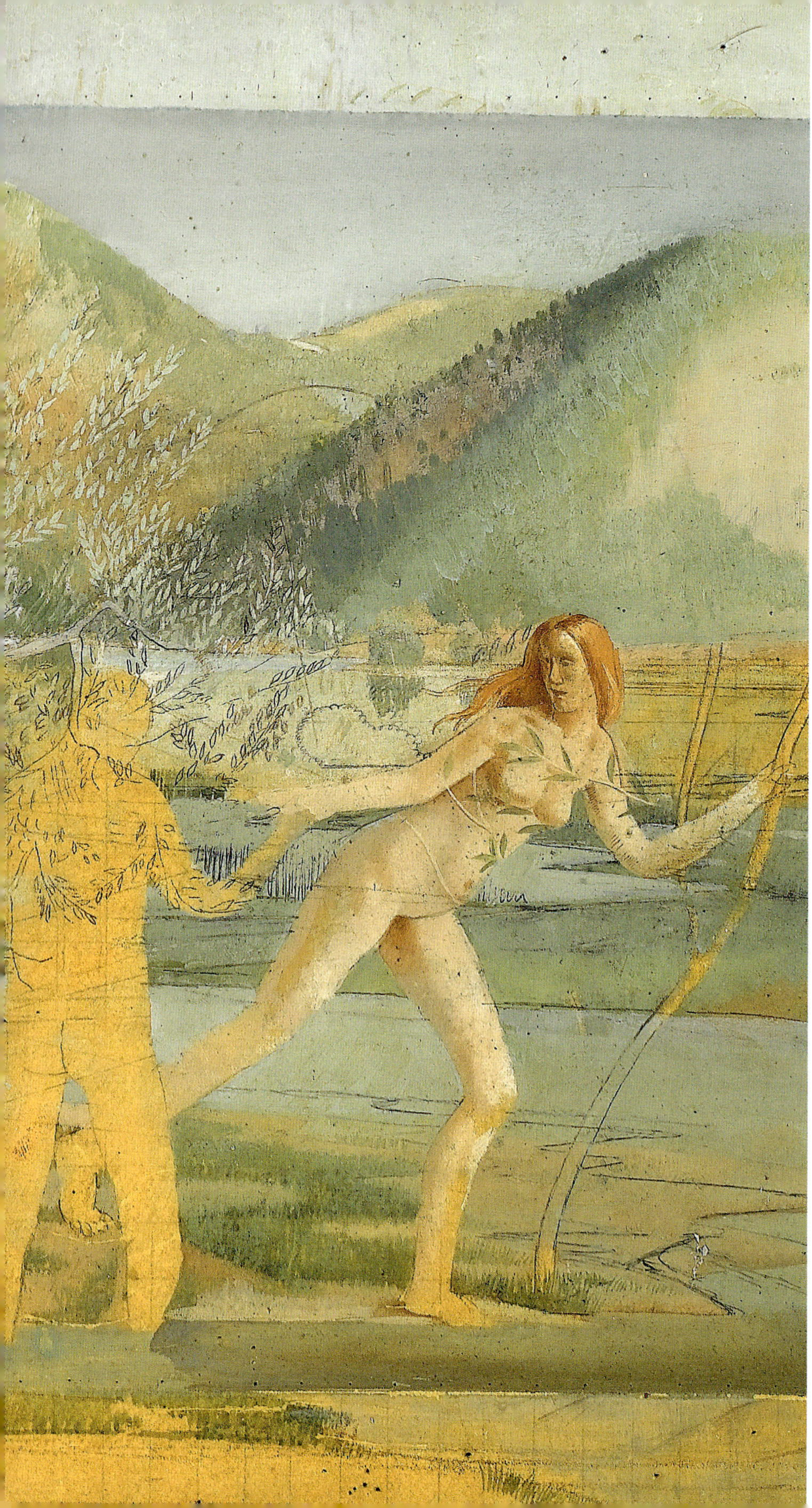

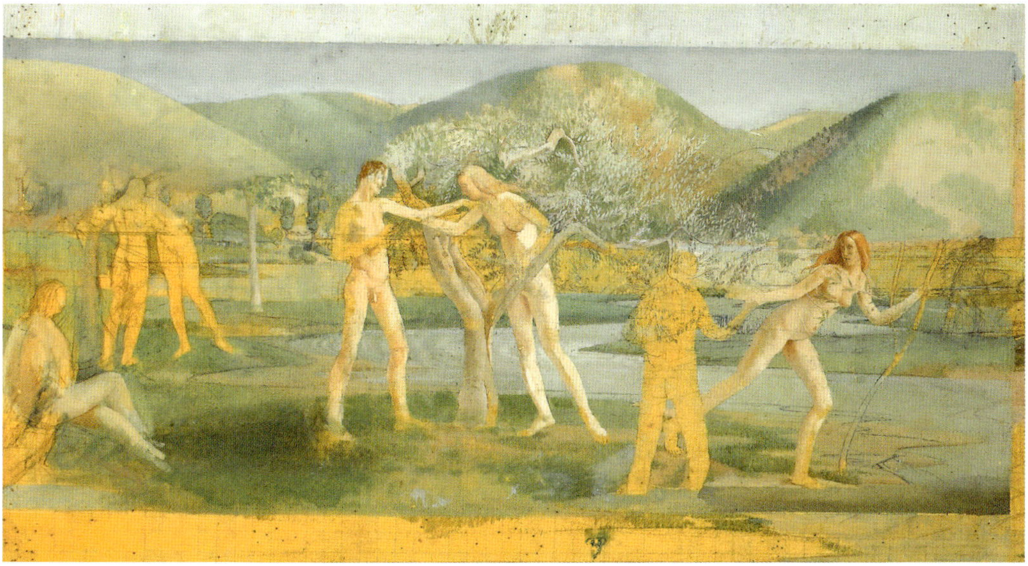

Sir Thomas Monnington (1902-1976)

Study for Allegory, circa 1924

Oil on tracing paper, laid on board - 31.7 x 57.2 cm.

Monnington's Allegory was the major work of his tenure as Rome Scholar in Decorative Painting. The cartoon and related studies which commenced in the Spring of 1924, occupied the larger part of the second year of Monnington's Scholarship. He began the execution of the painting, which was to occupy his third and final year, in March 1925. This small colour study is squared for transfer. The finished painting is in the collection of Tate Britain, having first been purchased in Rome by Jim Ede for the Contemporary Art Society.

The initial studies for Allegory were undertaken whilst Monnington and Knights were on their honeymoon in Lago di Piediluco – Knights serving as the inspiration for and model of the figures.

Asked in 1957 by the Tate to explain the title of his painting, Monnington stated that 'the whole design certainly had a very particular meaning and purpose and was an attempt to express in pictorial form my attitude to life – almost my faith'. Iconographically it contains elements of several myths but most obviously The Garden of Love; specific episodes within the painting are reminiscent of Adam and Eve; Apollo and Daphne; The Fountain of Youth.

Sir Thomas Monnington (1902-1976)

Portrait of Winifred Knights, circa 1931

Tempera over pen and ink on canvas - 36 x 28 cm.

Having enrolled at the Slade in 1918, at the age of 15, Monnington rapidly emerged as one of Tonks' star pupils, winning the Slade Prize for Head Drawing in 1922 and in the same year the Rome Scholarship in Decorative Painting. Whilst in Italy he married his fellow Slade student and Rome Scholar Winifred Knights.

This portrait in profile – in tempera over pen and ink - dates to the early 1930s after Knights and Monnington had returned to England. At the time they were living in Crawley Down, West Sussex whilst Monnington was working on his Supper at Emmaus altarpiece, with which this work has stylistic affinities. Charles Ricketts praised his work as being 'keenly alive to the merit of the Masterpieces he had seen in Italy and alive to the technical practices of the Masters', adding that 'studies Monnington has made... are characterized by the utmost thoroughness and care and are quite notable in their sense of finish and beauty'.

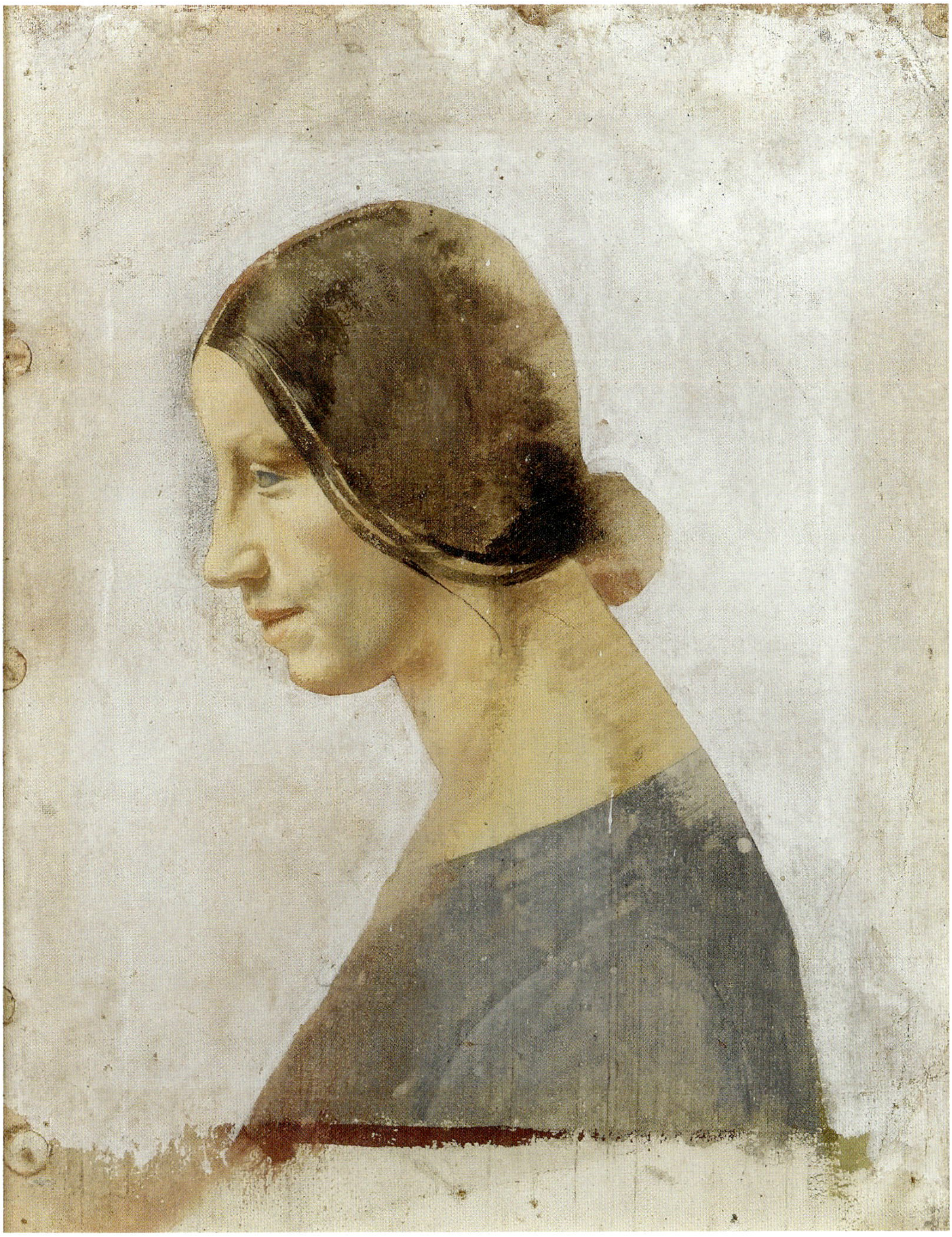

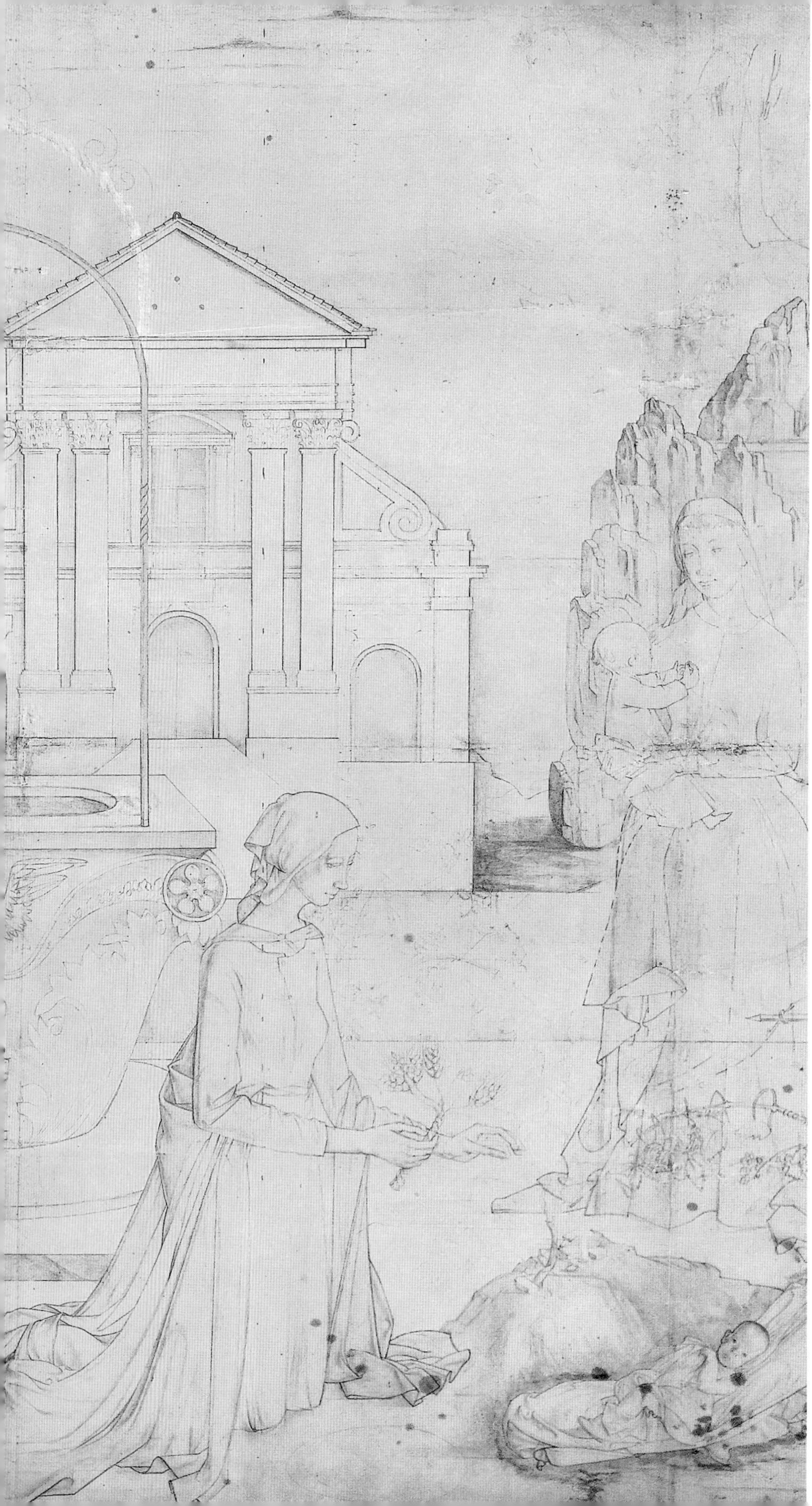

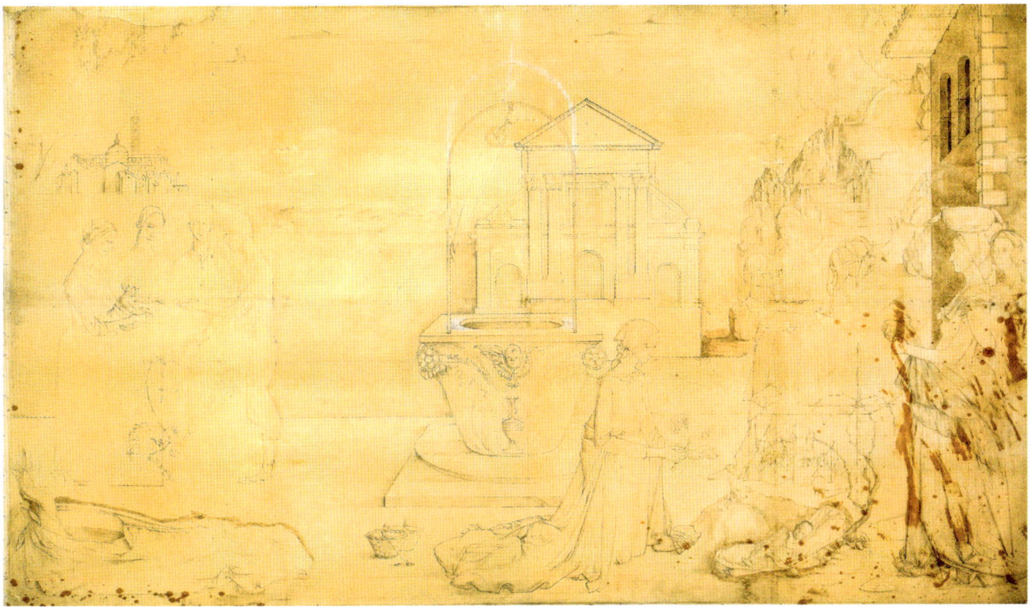

Anne Newland (1913-1997)

The legend of Ceres, circa 1938-39

Pencil and wash with splashes of ink on tracing paper, squared - 114.5 x 191 cm.

This full-size cartoon was Anne Newland's principal work during her Scholarship at the British School at Rome, which she was awarded in 1938. In correspondence with the Secretary of the School she described it as the central panel of a triptych for which she never intended to produce the side panels. The composition shows the influence of Andrea Mantegna whose works she was especially drawn to.

Ceres, according to ancient Roman myth, was the goddess of agriculture, grain crops, fertility and motherly relationships. Newland returned to the same composition ten years later in a related pencil drawing entitled Composition, *The Legend of Ceres*, (1949). In 1950, at The Royal Academy, Newland exhibited a variation on the theme, entitled Three Marys, which was loosely inspired by this earlier decorative composition.

Alan Sorrell (1904-1974)

Self portrait, nov. 1928

Pencil, ink and white gouache - 55.2 x 37 cm.

Sorrell undertook this self-portrait one month after he had arrived in Rome to take up his two-year scholarship, and it shows him in his downstairs studio at the British School. The self-portrait makes a bold statement and the quality of draughtsmanship and commanding composition make it one of the most striking works that Sorrell produced in Rome. The intensely observed and sharply delineated drawing of the folds and other forms demonstrate a study of Masaccio and Piero della Francesca and other Renaissance masters such as Durer. Sorrell's presentation of himself is introspective and melancholic, reflecting his state of mind during these early days in Rome.

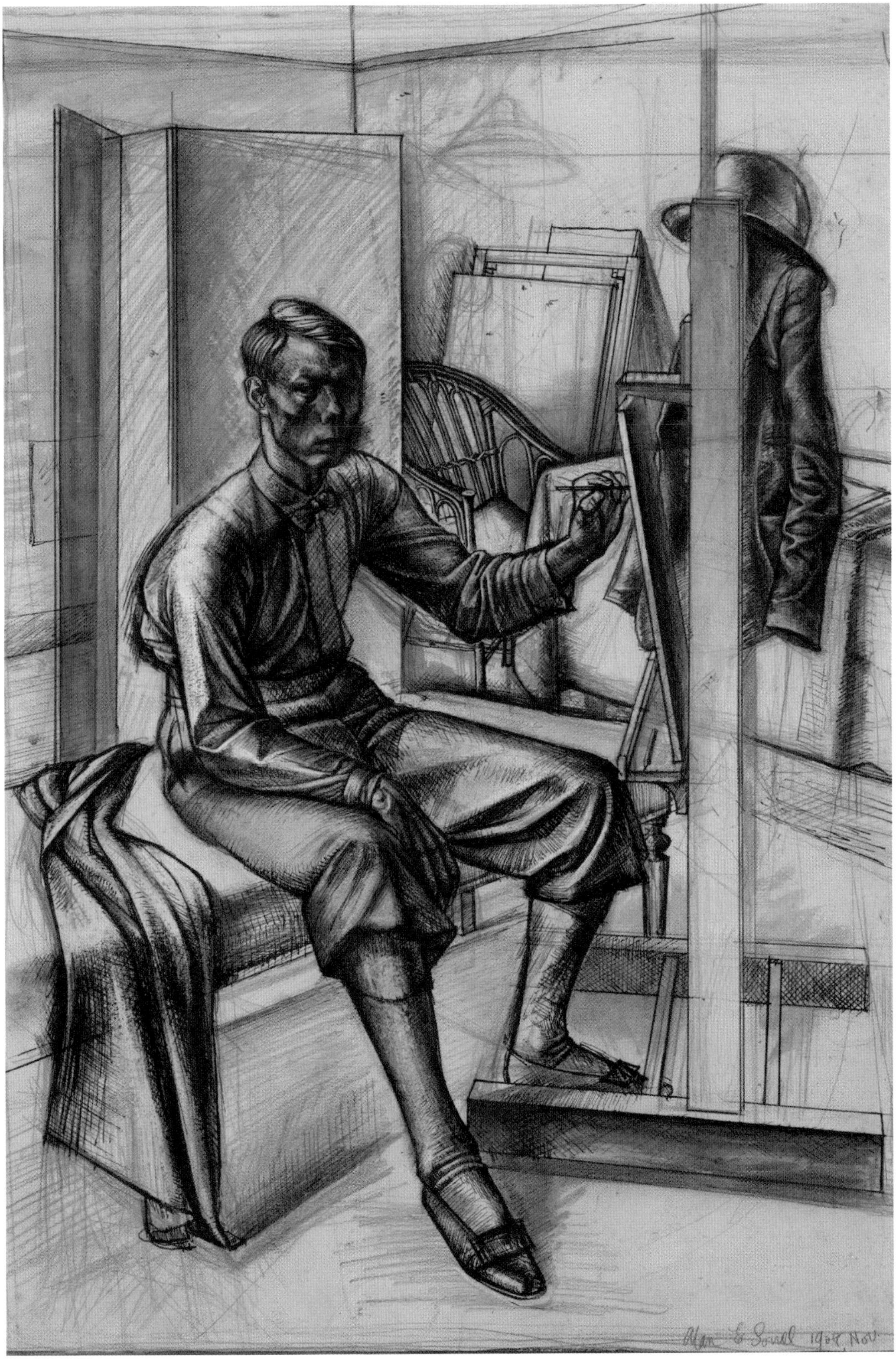

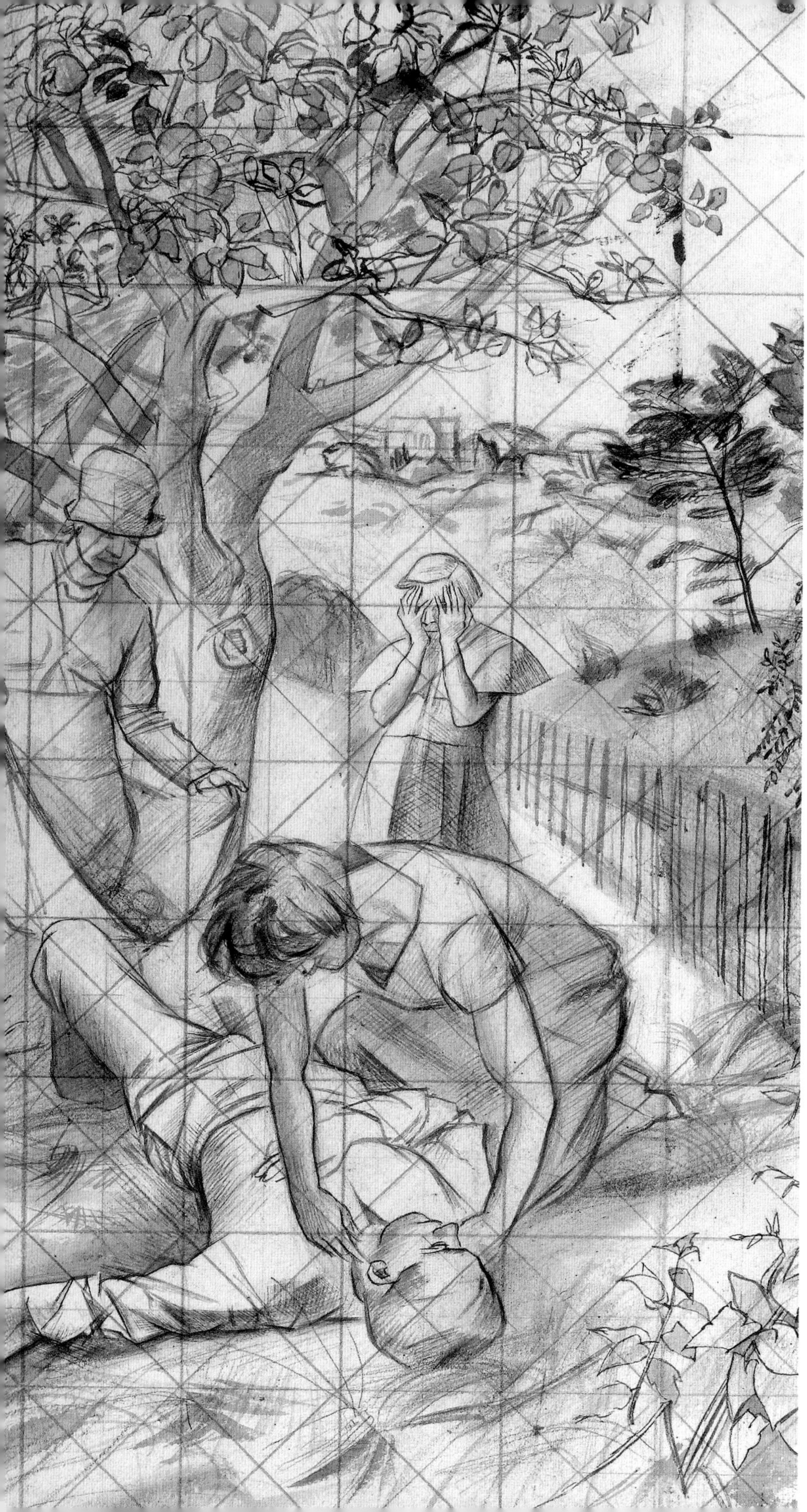

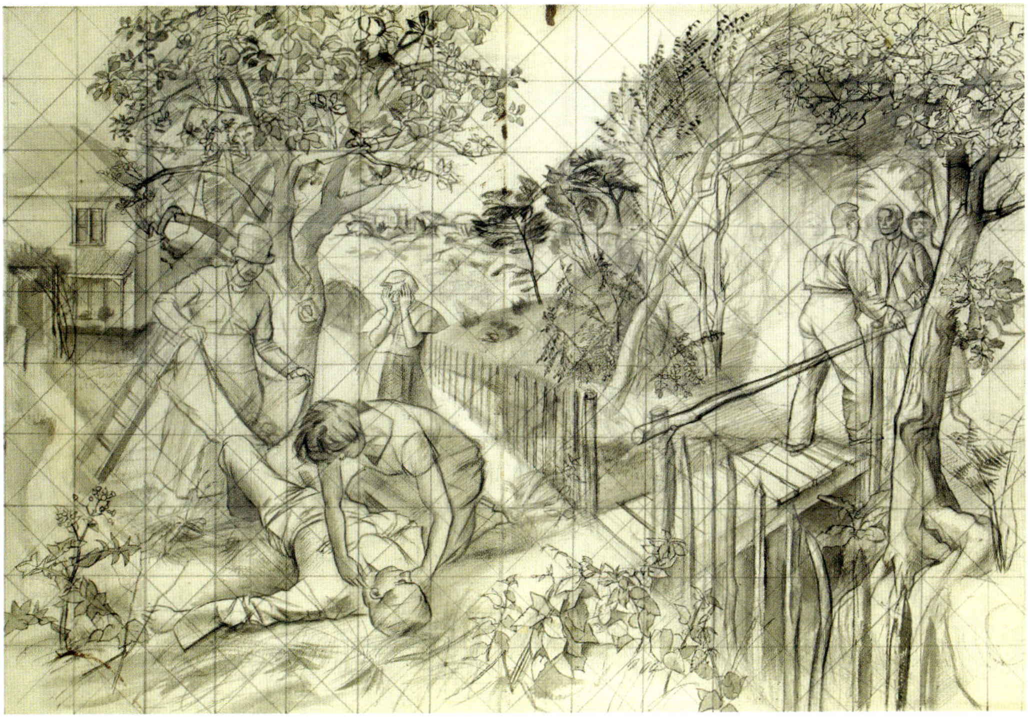

Alan Sorrell (1904-1974)

Study for The Long Journey, 1936

Pencil, pen and ink and wash, squared for transfer - 37 x 52.3 cm.

One of Sorrell's most evocative compositions, The Long Journey, exemplifies many of the qualities associated with Neo-Romantic movement which flowered during the interwar period. The narrative both engages and unsettles the viewer - the composition suggests that more of the story is unfolding beyond the confines of the space into which the viewer peers but cannot see beyond.

Richard Sorrell, the artist's son has described The Long Journey as follows: '*This carefully planned, double-focussed composition shows a domestic tragedy. The path leads across the bridged ditch in a sweep that suggests the journey from birth to the afterlife. The powerfully drawn trees and plants are, like those in The Artist in the Campagna, drawn from Nature. The title is inspired by E.M.Forster's 1907 The Longest Journey, the journey through life in a loveless marriage, and this is at least in part the subject of the book.*'

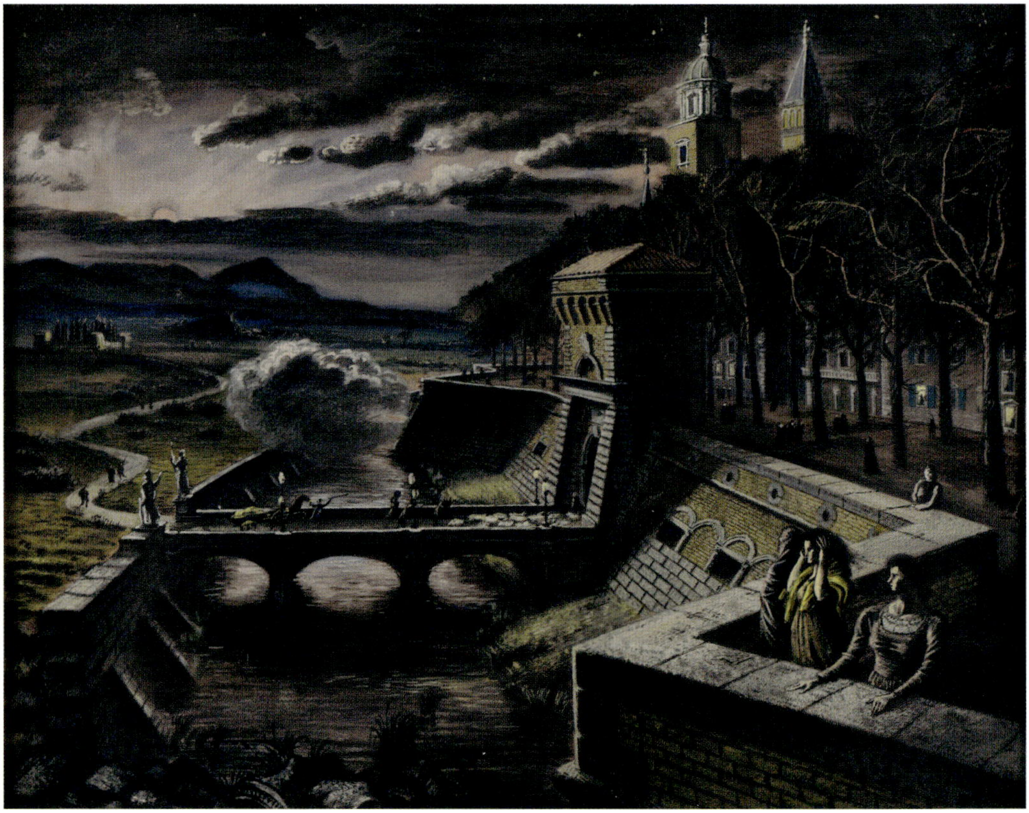

Alan Sorrell (1904-1974)

The Evening Signal, 1940

Signed, dated and title, pen and ink and gouache - 59 x 63 cm.

The composition of The Evening Signal has much in common with the archaeological reconstruction drawings for which Sorrell was best known at this period, many of which were published in the Illustrated London News. The Evening Signal was painted just before Sorrell joined the R.A.F, following the closure of the Royal College of Art, and an unsuccessful application to be a war artist. The painting conveys a deeply melancholic mood and possibly relates in part to the failure of Sorrell's marriage at this time.

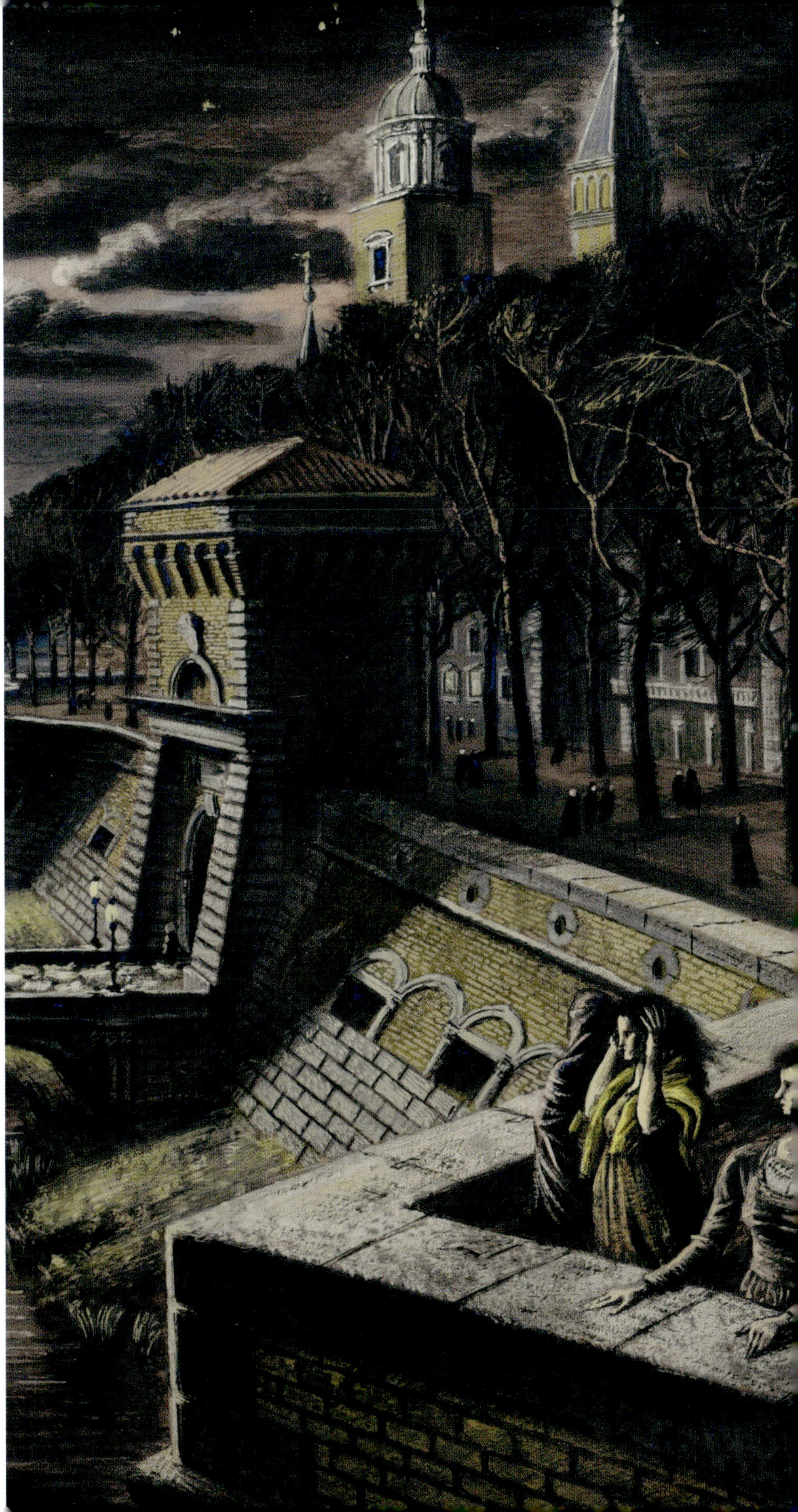

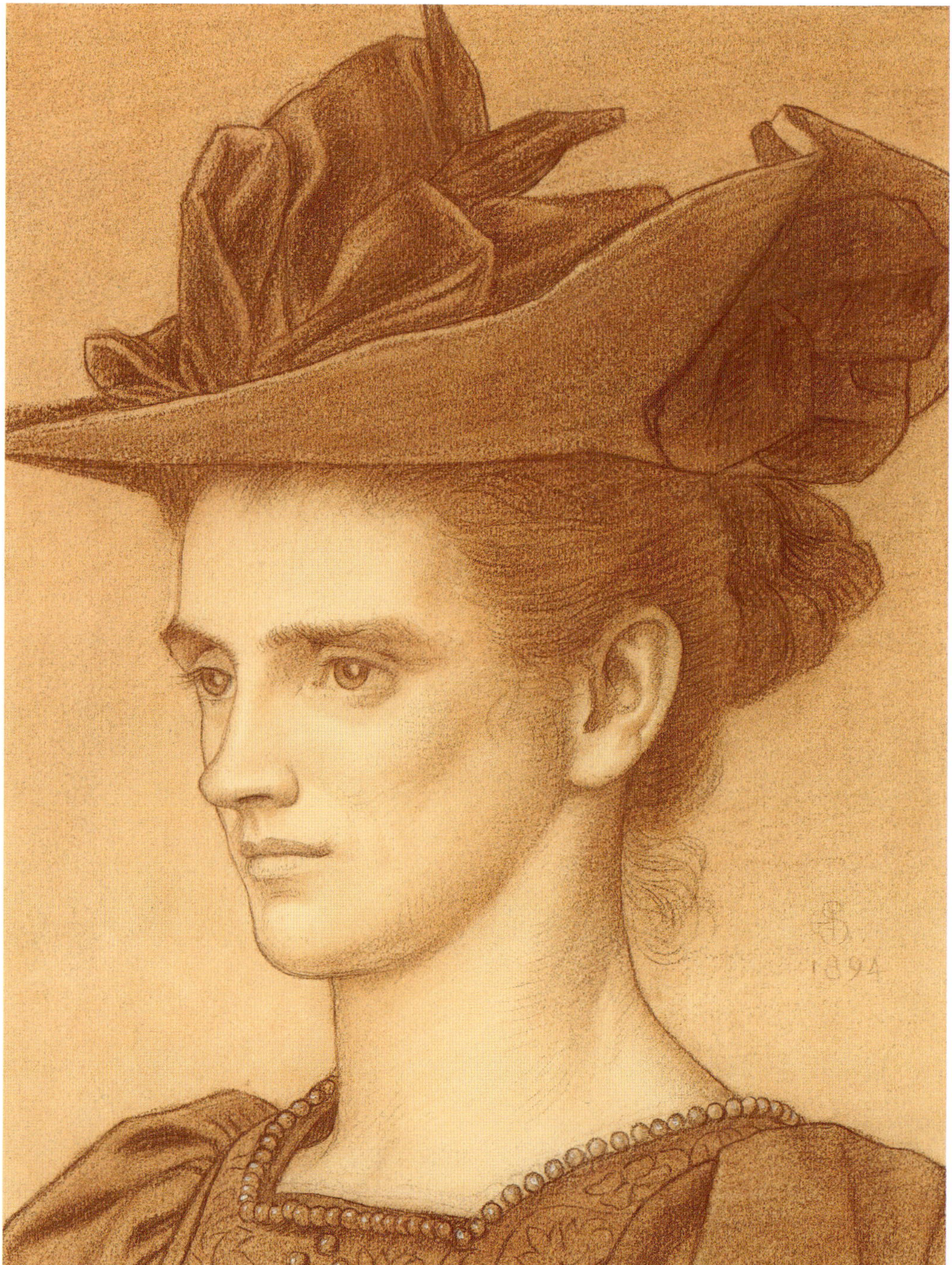
1894

Joseph Southall (1861-1944)

Anna Elizabeth Baker (study for The Coral Necklace), 1894

Signed with monogram and dated, red chalk heightened with white
25.5 x 18.4 cm.

Joseph Southall excelled as a draftsman, especially in red chalk and studies of this nature were often used to then produce paintings - as is the case here, a tempera panel of the same composition appearing a year later. Anna Elizabeth Baker - known as Bessie - became Southall's wife in 1903, the marriage was delayed for a number of years out of a sense of propriety because they were first cousins. She appears in many of Southall's pictures, including his celebrated double portrait The Agate (1911), in the collection of The National Portrait Gallery. Baker was an accomplished gilder and was responsible for the design of many of the Arts and Crafts designed by Southall.

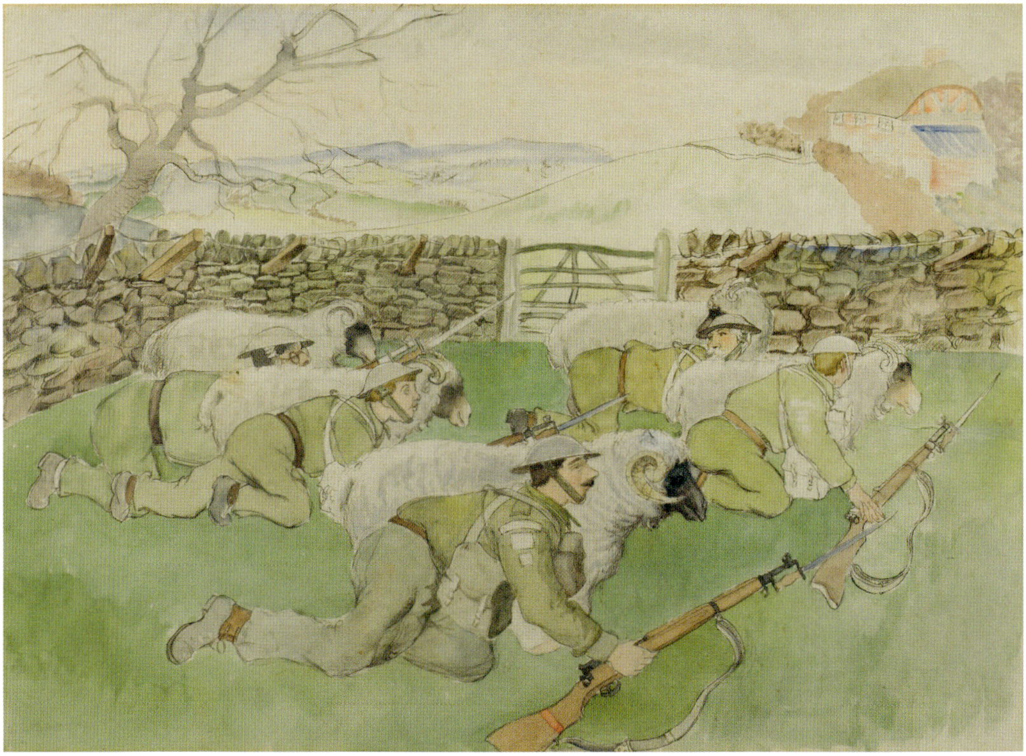

Gilbert Spencer (1892-1979)

Protective Covering, 1941

Pencil, pen, ink and watercolour - 55 x 73 cm.

Spencer was commissioned to produce paintings for the War Artists' Advisory Committee (WAAC) in 1940, 1942, 1943 and 1944.

From 1941 he taught at the Royal College of Art, which had been evacuated to Ambleside in the Lake District. Too old to serve in the army Spencer was active in the Home Guard as a subsection leader. His witty observations of life in the Home Guard were captured in a series of fourteen large watercolours. Intended for publication, the project had to be abandoned after the watercolours were intercepted by the Royal Mail, on their way to the printers, and, as an act of censorship, ripped along one side (subsequently repaired by Spencer).

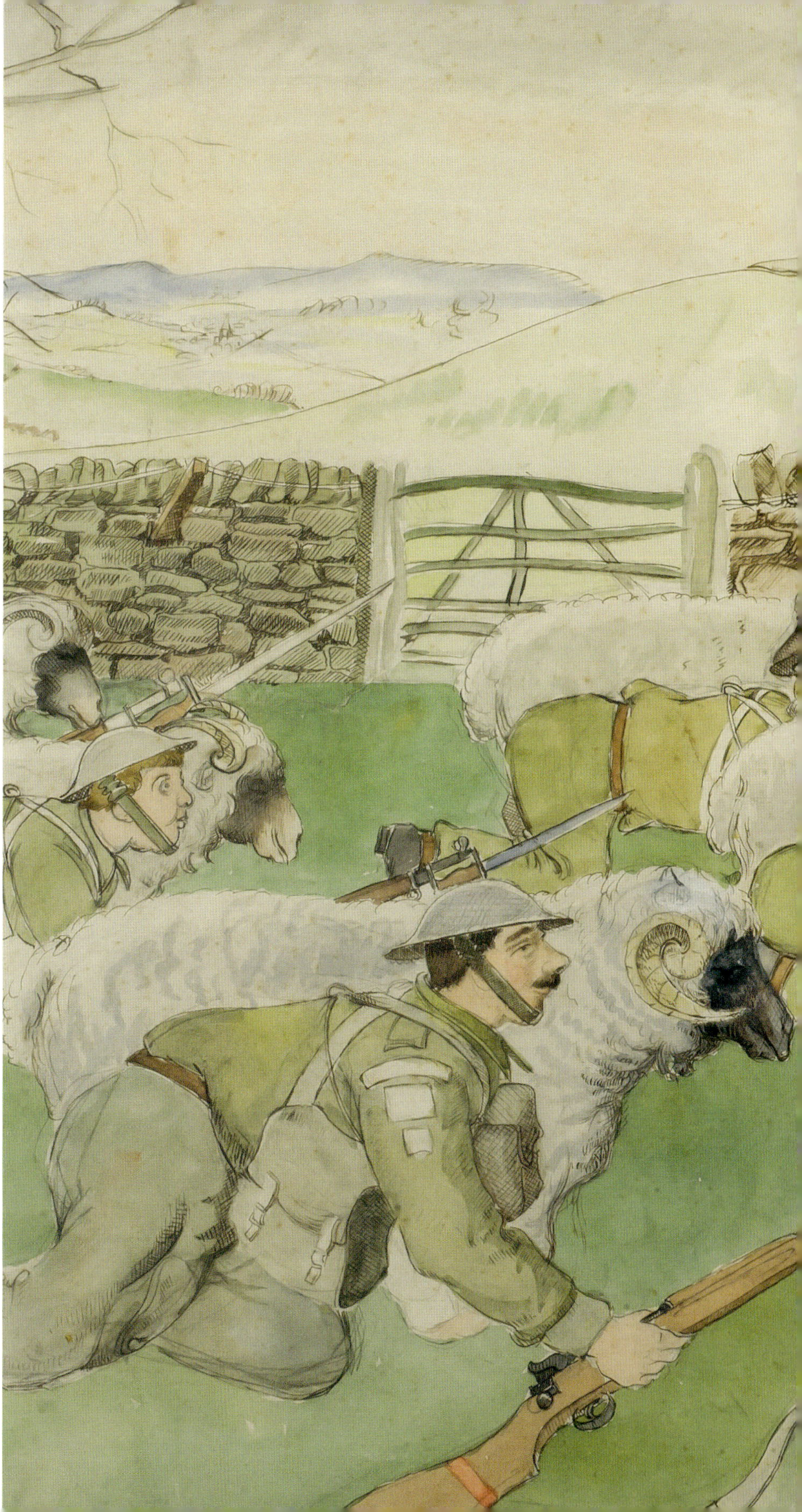

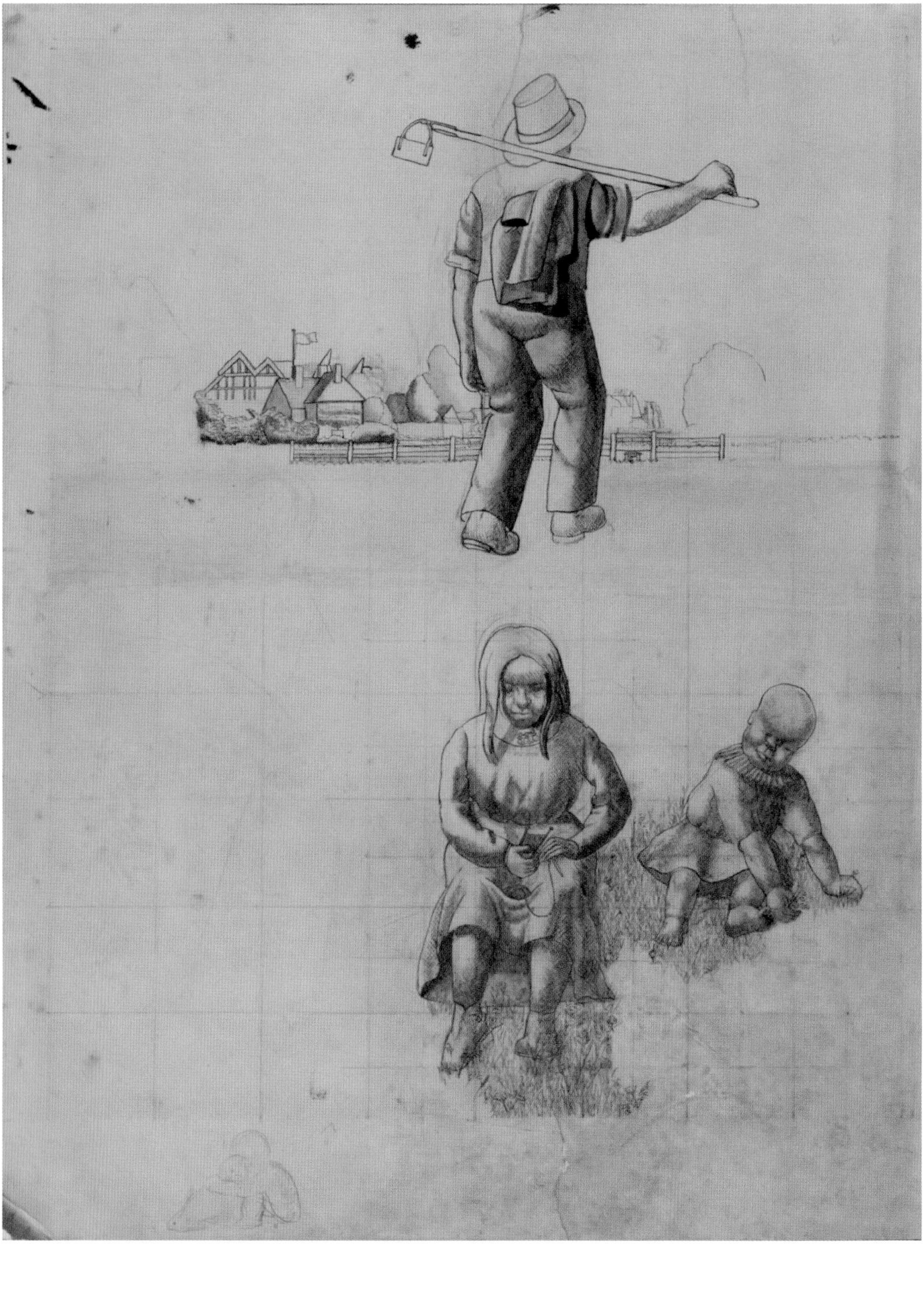

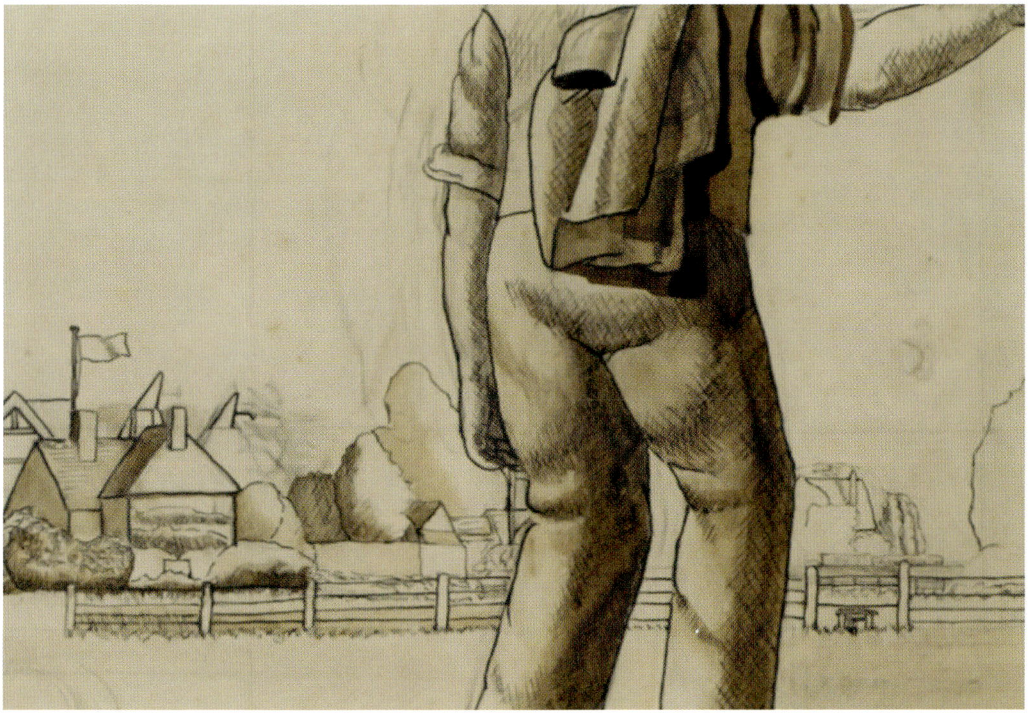

Gilbert Spencer (1892-1979)

Study for The Seven Ages of Man/ Summer

Pen, ink and pencil - 50 x 40 cm.

Gilbert Spencer won the Slade Summer Composition Competition of 1914 with his oil painting The Seven Ages of Man. According to Emma Chambers, 'Students were given a set title taken either from literary sources such as the Bible or the classics, or themes such as 'bathers' or 'labourers', and required to compose large-scale paintings which placed groups of figures in a setting. Allied to the tradition of History painting, central to academic art training from the seventeenth century, this competition gave the students considerable scope for exploring different models of narrative painting.' Spencer's composition is set in his home village of Cookham, the Crown Inn visible in the background.

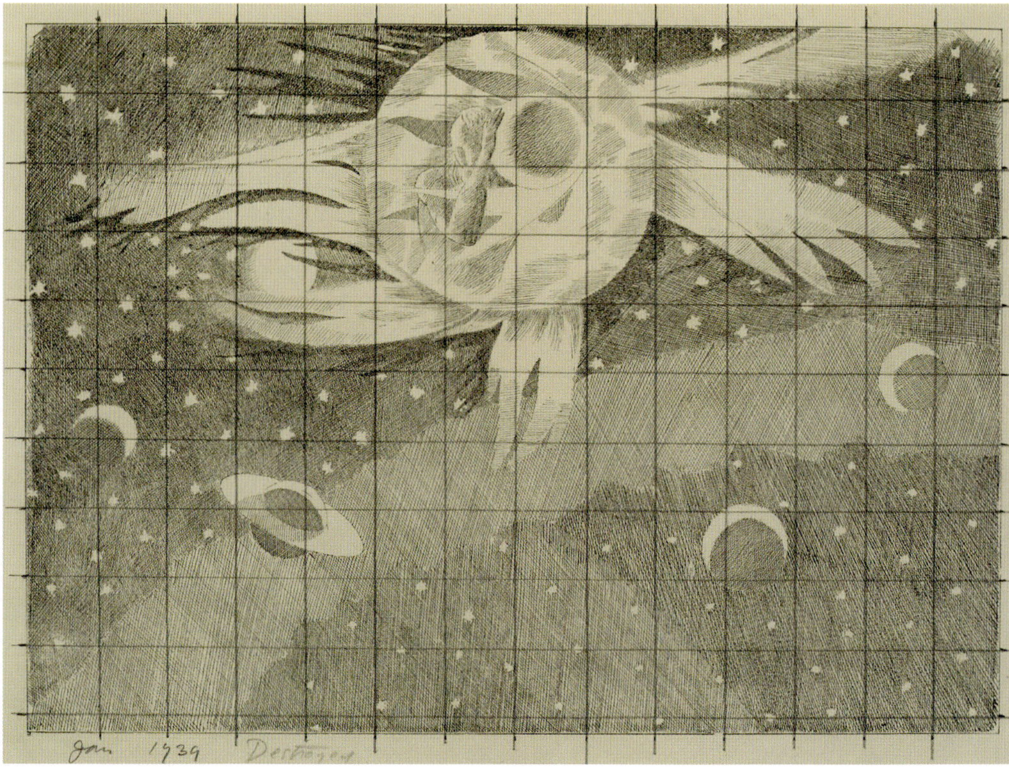

Gilbert Spencer (1892-1979)

God Creating the World, 1934

Original proof, squared in ink with pencil notes to margin - 28.3 x 37.4 cm.

Spencer produced a series of drawings to illustrate The Ten Commandments in the early 1930's – these were published by the Mill House Press in 1934, in the form of tipped-in lithographic plates. Squaring up in pen and ink a set of proofs from the published edition, Spencer appears to have had the intention of later creating oil paintings based on the drawings.

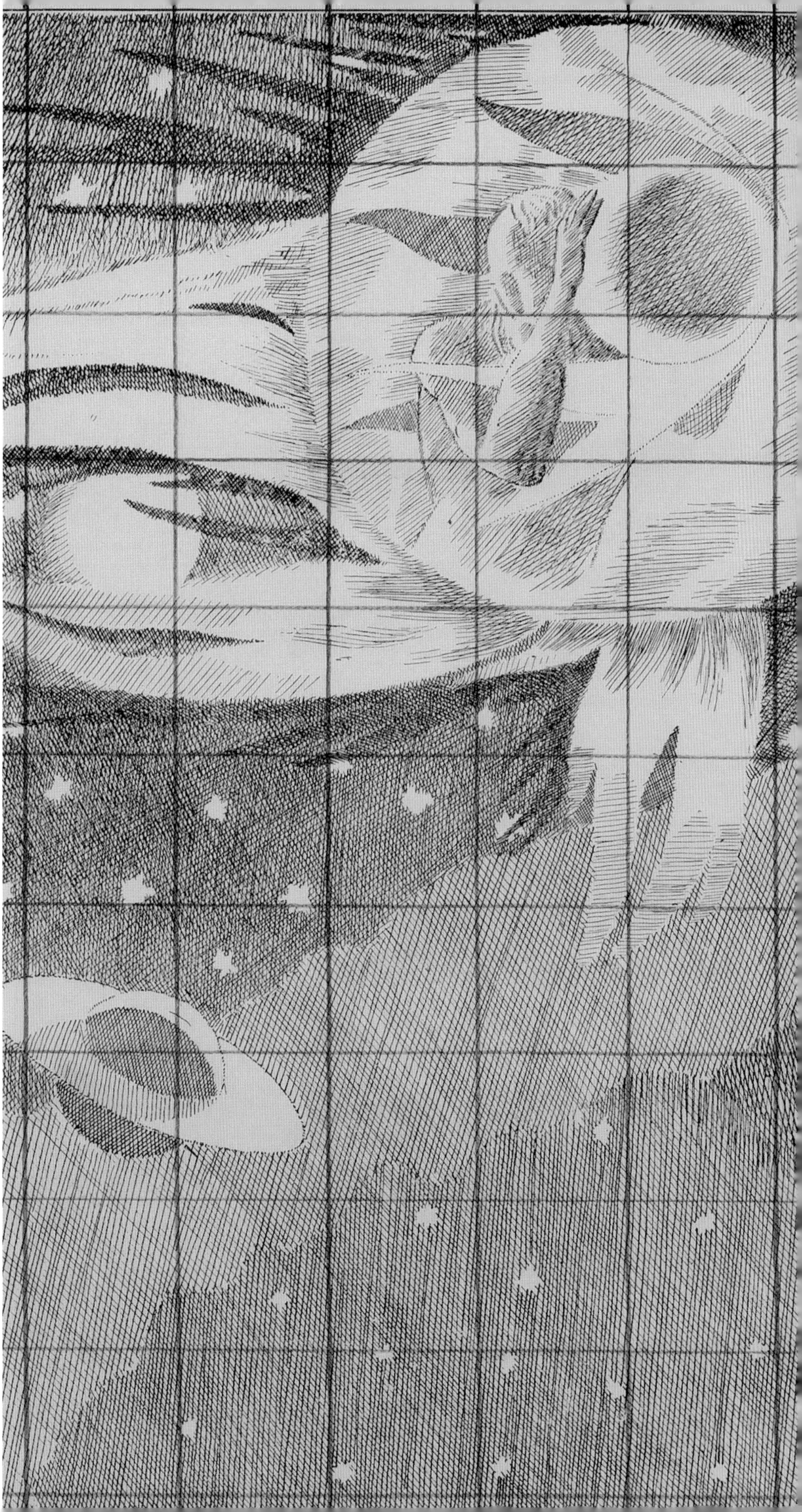

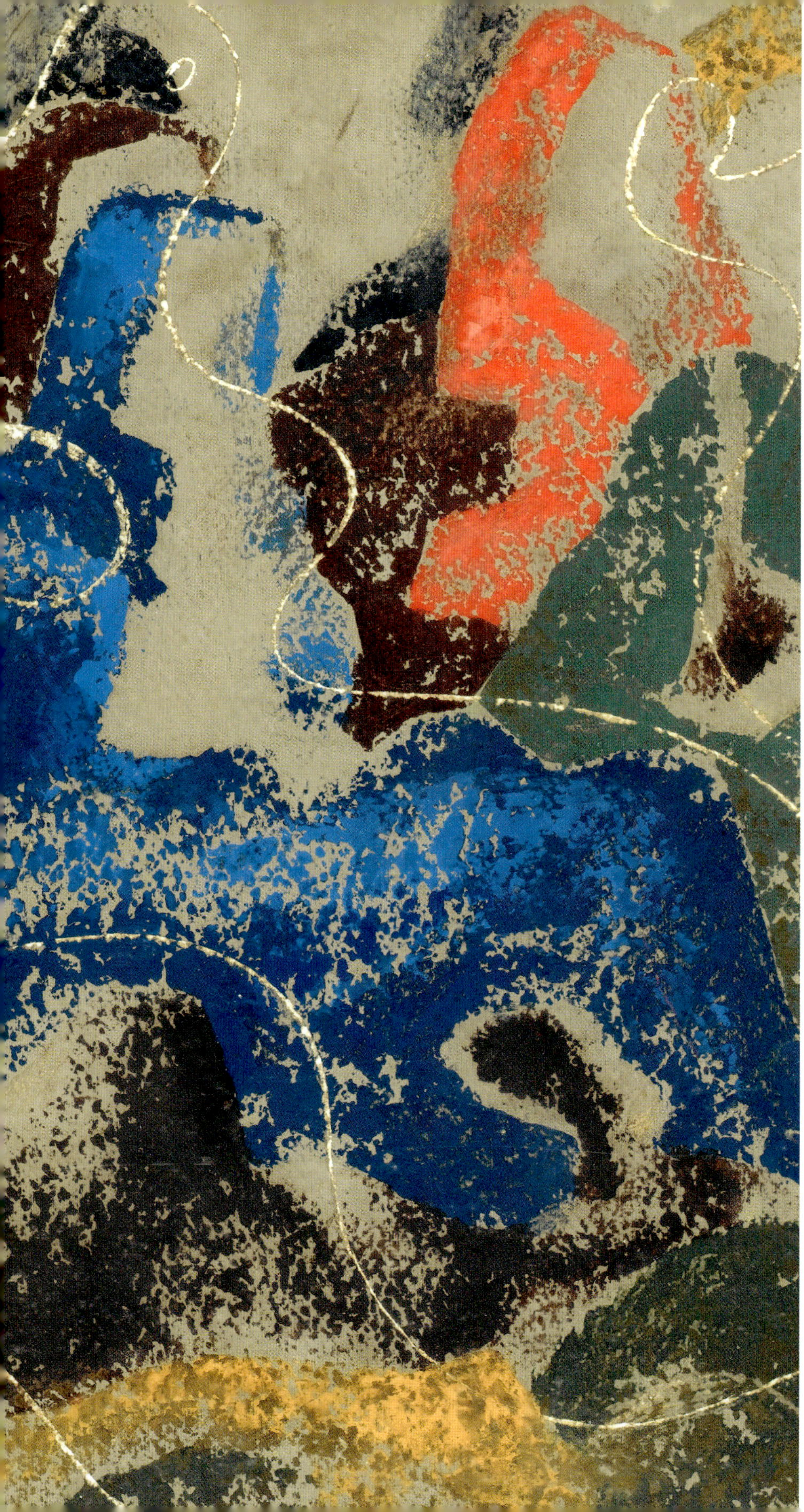

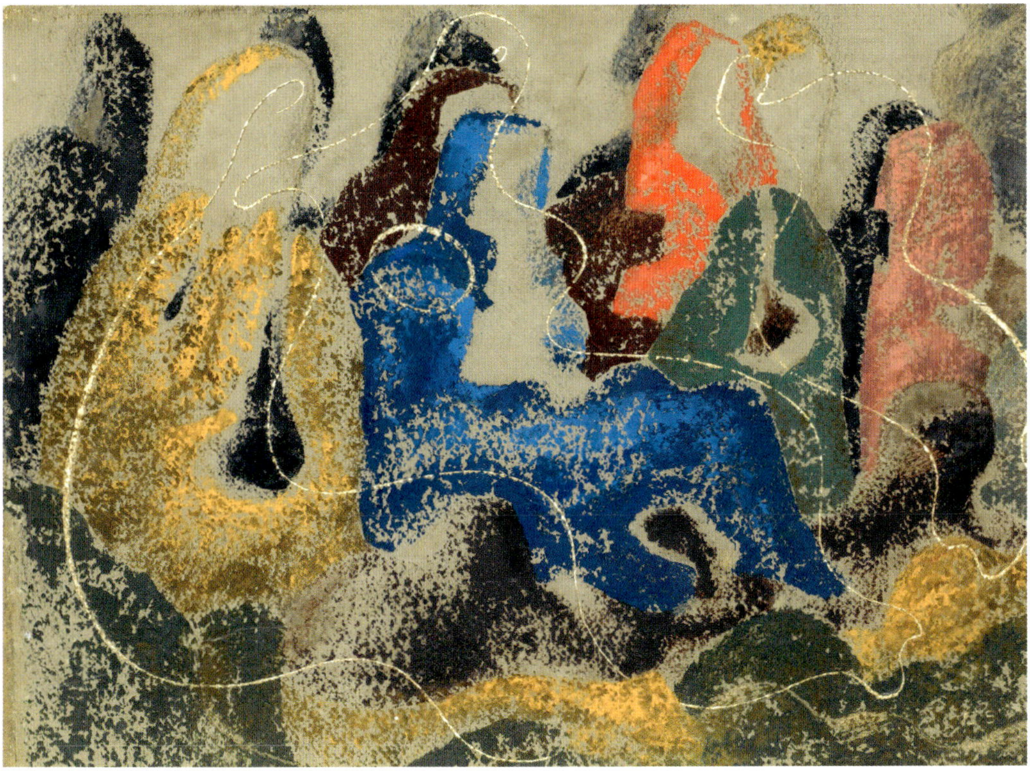

John Cecil Stephenson (1889-1965)

Madonna of the Rocks, circa 1945

Oil on paper with scratching out - 40.7 x 53.3 cm.

Exhibited: London, Drian Gallery, 22 November - 23 December 1966, no 54

The influence of Barbara Hepworth and Henry Moore - Stephenson's neighbours at The Mall Studios in Hampstead in the late 1930's and early 1940's – is evident in this wartime composition. The painting is also likely to have been inspired by Leonardo Da Vinci's celebrated composition of the same title, in the National Gallery, London, that shows the Virgin Mary with Saint John the Baptist and an angel. The innovative painting techniques used by Leonardo give the impression that the figures are emerging from the darkness. Stephenson's use of oil, with scratching out, applied to a dark-coloured texture paper, replicates a similar luminous effect.

William Strang (1859-1921)

Seated Nude (reclining, three quarter view), circa 1890

Silverpoint - 55 x 41 cm.

An artist working in metal point uses a sharp, pointed instrument (a stylus) with a metal tip to draw on paper, parchment, or wood those has been specially coated. As the stylus, which can be gold or silver, travels across this slightly abrasive ground, a small amount of metal is scraped off and remains behind, creating a line.

William Strang was taught metal point by Alphonse Legros (1837-1911), Professor of Drawing at the Slade, one of the chief exponents in the resurgence of this medium during the second half of the 19th century. (Strang would become the assistant master in Legros' etching class). The medium was perfectly suited to the subtlety and technical quality of Strang's draughtsmanship.

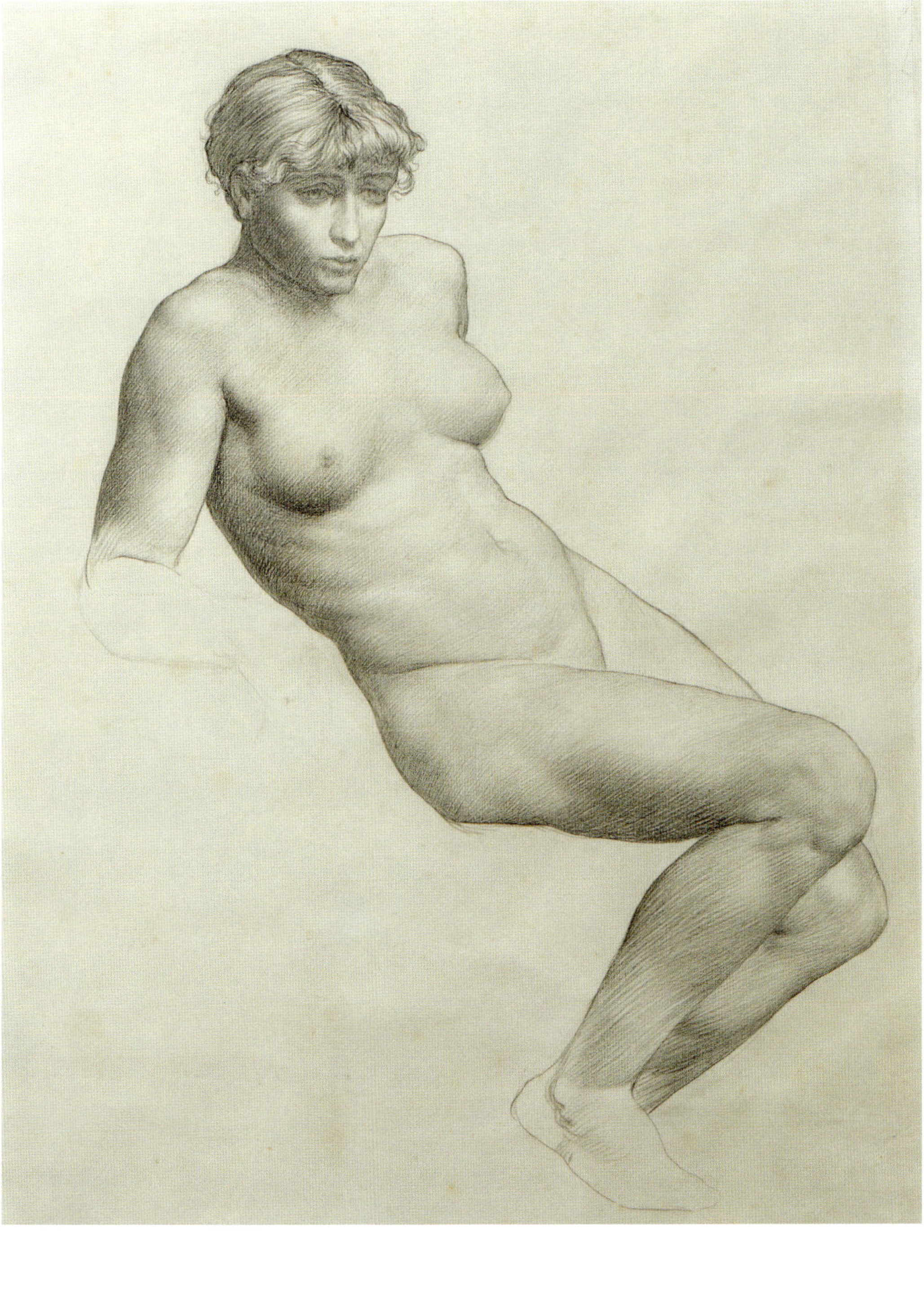

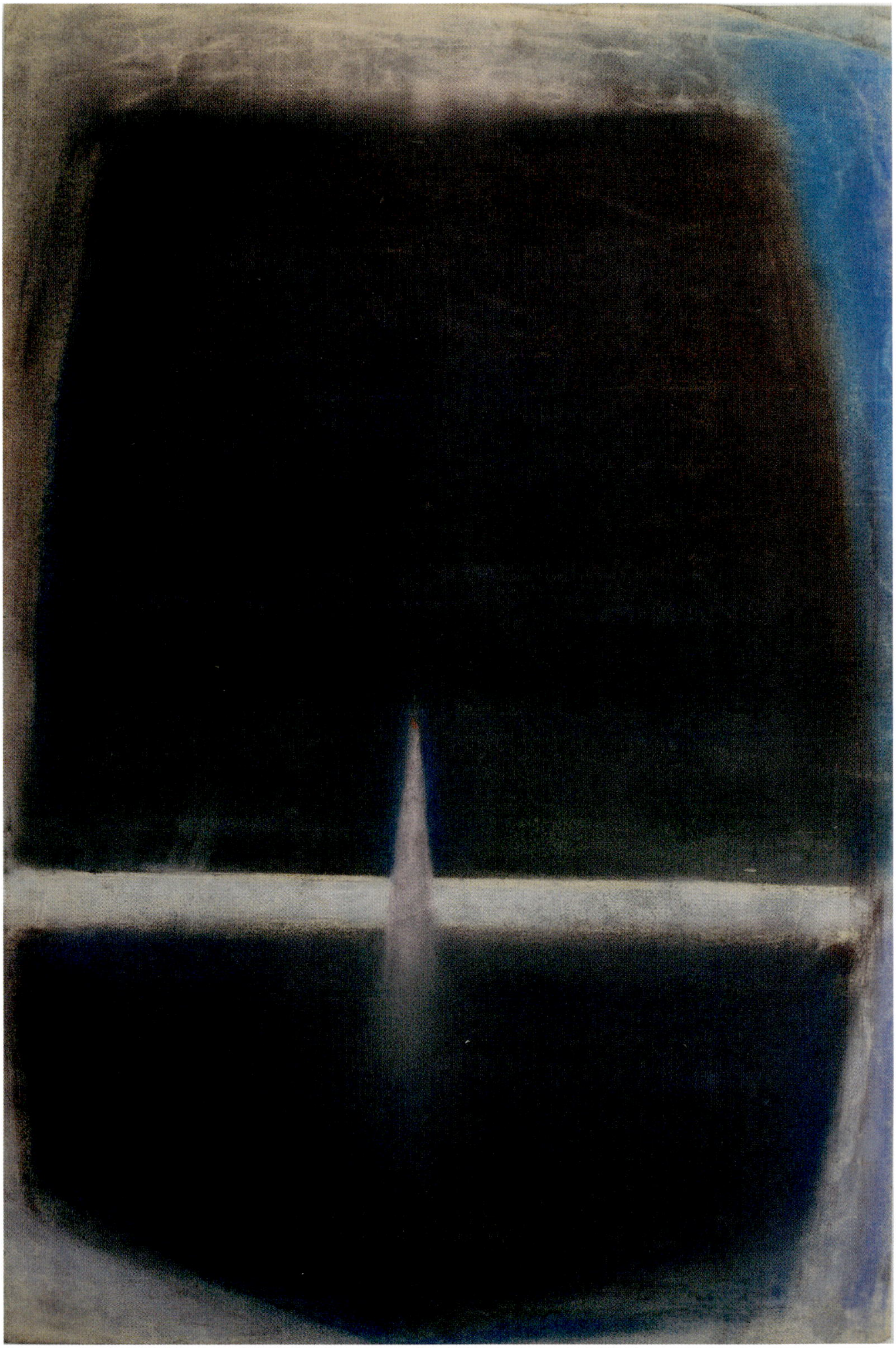

John Tunnard (1900-1971)

Celestial Light, circa 1950

Coloured chalk - 54.5 x 37.4 cm.

Semi-abstract shapes which bring to mind distant horizons, the sea, moons, stars, planets, birds in flight, trees and skeletal forms characterise much of Tunnard's oeuvre. This was especially so in the case of Tunnard's 30 foot long Crystal Forms mural, created for the Festival of Britain in 1951 and displayed in the Regatta Restaurant on the South Bank, London, (now destroyed).

In her autobiography, Peggy Guggenheim described his colour as '*exquisite: I was happy to think that I had discovered a genius.*'

Tunnard's compositions, with their Neo-Romantic sensibility, are often compared to that of Graham Sutherland. In later life he became interested in space travel, depicting satellites and moonscapes in his paintings.

Drawings 1990-2022
will be on exhibition at:

Purdy Hicks Gallery
25 Thurloe Street
London SW7 2LQ
7 - 29 October 2022.

Gillian Ayres	Laila Tara H
Olga Chernysheva	Waqas Khan
Jonathan Delafield Cook	Elizabeth Magill
Mark Francis	Nina Murdoch

Acknowledgements
We are especially grateful to Rebecca Hicks, Nicola Shane and Siena Hicks of Purdy Hicks and to Alistair Hicks.
We would like to thank Richard Shepherd at his team at Sotheran's. We are also indebted again to Geoff Hassell of Artboigs.co.uk. We would like to thank Clémence Godinot for her outstanding catalogue design.
We would also like to acknowledge the following:
George Breeze, Christopher Campbell-Howes, Devon Cox, Dr Gill Clarke,Daniel Dullaway, Nicholas Finney, Paul Gough, Nicolas Granger-Taylor, Glyn Hopkins, Tudor Hopkins, Dr Libby Horner, George Kenney, Anton Liss, Eva Liss, Maudji Llewellyn, Pauline Lucas, Conor Mullan, Alan Powers, Peyton Skipwith, Julie Wheelwright.

Index